IMAGES OF WAR

THE BATTLE OF OKINAWA 1945

THE PACIFIC WAR'S LAST INVASION

RARE PHOTOGRAPHS FROM WARTIME ARCHIVES

Jon Diamond

Pen & Sword
MILITARY

First published in Great Britain in 2019 by
PEN & SWORD MILITARY
An imprint of
Pen & Sword Books Ltd
47 Church Street
Barnsley
South Yorkshire
S70 2AS

ISBN 978-1-52672-600-1

Typeset by Concept, Huddersfield, West Yorkshire, HD4 5JL.
Printed and bound in India by Replika Press Pvt. Ltd.

Pen & Sword Books Limited incorporates the imprints of Atlas, Archaeology, Aviation, Discovery, Family History, Fiction, History, Maritime, Military, Military Classics, Politics, Select, Transport, True Crime, Air World, Frontline Publishing, Leo Cooper, Remember When, Seaforth Publishing, The Praetorian Press, Wharncliffe Local History, Wharncliffe Transport, Wharncliffe True Crime and White Owl.

For a complete list of Pen & Sword titles please contact
PEN & SWORD BOOKS LIMITED
47 Church Street, Barnsley, South Yorkshire S70 2AS, England
E-mail: enquiries@pen-and-sword.co.uk
Website: www.pen-and-sword.co.uk

Contents

Acknowledgements **4**

Abbreviations **5**

Chapter One

Strategic Prelude to the Campaign for Okinawa **7**
Map: Strategic prelude 8
Map: The Pacific War, September 1944–April 1945 14

Chapter Two

Terrain, Fortifications and Weapons **50**
Map: Okinawa and surrounding islands 51

Chapter Three

Commanders and Combatants **119**

Chapter Four

US Tenth Army's Amphibious Assault on Okinawa **160**
Map: Landing (L)-Day: Invasion of Okinawa on 1 April 1945 161

Chapter Five

**Tenth Army Advance and the Protracted Conquest
of Okinawa** **181**
Map: Inland and offshore Tenth Army advances 182
Map: Assault on the 'Naha-Shuri' Line 188
Map: US Tenth Army attack on IJA 32nd Army's final redoubts. . . 196

Epilogue **219**

References **229**

Acknowledgements

This archival photograph volume in the *Images of War* series is dedicated to the armed forces service members who fought, were wounded and perished during the Okinawa campaign – 'the last battle'. We ponder upon viewing these photographs about the heroic sacrifice made to maintain freedom, lest we forget. The author is indebted to the able assistance of the archivists at both the United States Army Military History Institute (USAMHI) at the United States Army War College in Carlisle, Pennsylvania and the Still Photo Section of the National Archives and Records Administration (NARA) in College Park, Maryland. Their diligence is much appreciated as they maintain and safeguard these historic images.

Abbreviations

AA – Anti-aircraft
AAA – Anti-aircraft artillery
AIF – Australian Imperial Force
AP – Armour-piercing
AT – Anti-tank
BAR – Browning automatic rifle
C-in-C – Commander-in-Chief
CINCPOA – Commander-in-Chief, Pacific Ocean Areas
CNO – Chief of Naval Operations
COS – Chief of Staff
CPA – Central Pacific Area
CSA – Confederate States of America
ETO – European Theatre of Operations
GMC – Gun motor carriage
HE – High explosive
HMC – Howitzer motor carriage
HMG – Heavy machine gun
IJA – Imperial Japanese Army
IJN – Imperial Japanese Navy
IMB – Independent Mixed Brigade
LCI – Landing Craft Infantry
LCM – Landing Craft, Mechanised
LCVP – Landing Craft, Vehicle Personnel

LMG – Light machine-gun
LSM – Landing Ship Medium
LVT – Landing Vehicle Tracked
LVT(A) – Landing Vehicle Tracked (Armoured)
M&P – Military & police
MAG – Marine Air Groups
MAW – Marine Aircraft Wing
MMG – Medium machine-gun
OP – Observation post
PFC – Private First Class
SB – Stretcher-bearer
SMG – Sub-machine-gun
SNLF – Special Naval Landing Force
SPA – South Pacific Area
SWPA – South-west Pacific Area
TB – Tank Battalion
TD – Tank Destroyer
TF – Task Force
TNT – Tri Nitro Toluene
USMC – United States Marine Corps
USNR – United States Naval Reserve
IMAC – I Marine Amphibious Corps
IIIAC – III Amphibious Corps
VAC – V Amphibious Corps

Chapter One

Strategic Prelude to the Campaign for Okinawa

From December 1941 to June 1942, the Imperial Japanese Army (IJA) and Imperial Japanese Navy (IJN) were victorious across the Asian continent, the Philippine and Netherland East Indies Archipelagos, Malaya and Singapore, Hong Kong, New Britain, the northern coasts of North-east New Guinea and Papua as well as many island groups across the Central and South Pacific. Three seminal events heralded the Japanese *Blitzkrieg's* end. On 18 April 1942, US Army B-25B medium bombers from Vice-Admiral William F. 'Bull' Halsey's Task Force (TF)-16 comprising the American aircraft carriers USS *Hornet* and *Enterprise*, attacked Tokyo. Although little damage was done, the attack solidified the Imperial High Command's approval of Admiral Isoroku Yamamoto's plan to attack Midway Island and draw the American Pacific Fleet into a decisive surface battle. However, during the first week of May 1942, American and Japanese task forces duelled with carrier-based aircraft in the Battle of the Coral Sea. A Japanese amphibious invasion of Port Moresby, New Guinea, on Papua's southern coast as a possible stepping-stone to invade Australia's Northern Territories was thwarted. On 4–7 June 1942, the Battle of Midway concluded with a decisive victory for Rear-Admiral Raymond A. Spruance's carrier task forces, which sank four of Admiral Chūichi Nagumo's carriers. Imperial Japan's high tide began to ebb.

After discovering an airfield's construction on Guadalcanal, across from a Japanese sea-plane base on Tulagi in the Southern Solomon Islands, Admiral Ernest J. King, Commander-in-Chief (C-in-C) and Chief of Naval Operations (CNO) of the US Navy marshalled his forces to interdict the enemy's further south-eastward expansion. On 7 August 1942, Guadalcanal was amphibiously assaulted by the US 1st Marine Division (Reinforced), under the command of Major-General Alexander A. Vandegrift. A gruelling six-month Marine defence of Henderson Field's perimeter followed by the US Army's Americal and 25th Divisions' reinforcements punctuated horrific jungle combat, never-ending Japanese aerial attacks and deadly naval surface action. By the first week of February 1943, Japan evacuated Guadalcanal, ending their South-eastern Pacific strategy to sever the sea lanes to the Antipodes.

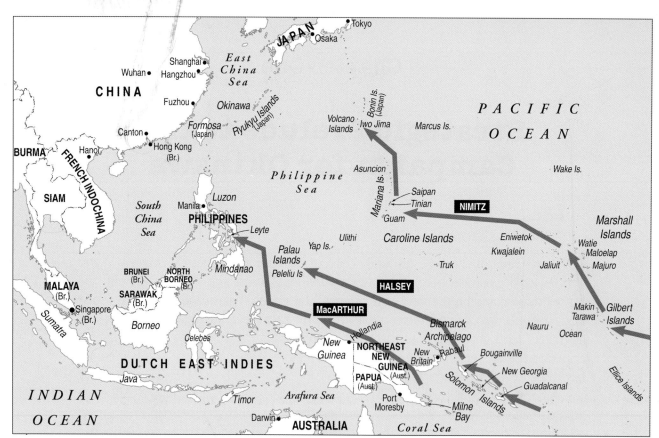

Strategic prelude: The Pacific War, August 1942–October 1944. From 7 December 1941 until late spring 1942, Japan conquered: the American territories of Wake Island, Guam, the Philippines; British-controlled Hong Kong, Malaya and Singapore, the Solomon and Gilbert Islands; the Australian-governed Bismarck Archipelago as well as the northern coast of Papua and North-east New Guinea and Nauru Island; and the Dutch East Indies. In addition, the Japanese had been strengthening their Mandates in the Northern Mariana, Marshall, Caroline and Palau groups. Following the US Navy strategic victories over IJN carrier task forces at the Coral Sea and Midway in May and June 1942, respectively, the Allies commenced a counter-offensive in the Pacific. American forces strengthened the South Pacific island chains south-east of the Solomon Islands and had landed on Funafuti in the British-controlled Ellice Islands in early October 1942. Prior to that, on 7 August 1942, Major-General Archer Vandegrift's 1st Marine Division (Reinforced) seized the Solomon Islands of Tulagi and Guadalcanal, the latter with its almost completed airfield. Concurrent with the US naval and ground forces defending Guadalcanal in an epic six-month struggle, Australia committed Militia battalions and, eventually, AIF veteran Middle East divisions to defend Port Moresby from an IJA over-land attack and from an amphibious assault at Milne Bay from August–September 1942. From October 1942 until early January 1943, MacArthur's Australian and American infantry forces wrested Buna, Gona and Sanananda Point in bloody advances along the northern Papuan coast.

In early 1943, three Allied axes of advance developed. In the CPA, Admiral Nimitz assigned, in August 1943, his COS Vice-Admiral Raymond Spruance to command the Central Pacific Force (re-designated Fifth Fleet in April 1944). This US Navy, Marine and Army force advanced on separate invasions and campaigns in the Gilbert Islands (November 1943), the Marshall Islands (January–February 1944), the Marianas (June–August 1944). After the seizure of the Marianas, Nimitz was

On 21 February 1942, President Franklin D. Roosevelt cabled General Douglas A. MacArthur on Corregidor and ordered him to leave for Australia. On 17 March, MacArthur and his retinue arrived at Batchelor Field, south of Darwin, in a fleet of battle-weary B-17s.

After seizing Rabaul on New Britain in late January 1942, the IJA and IJN landed units at Salamaua, Lae and Finschhafen on the Huon Gulf in North-east New Guinea from 8 March–7 April. In mid-July, Japanese Special Naval Landing Force (SNLF) troops landed at Buna, Gona and Sanananda, along the northern coast of Papua, the eastern third of New Guinea.

In June 1942, MacArthur, as C-in-C of the South-west Pacific Area (SWPA), dispatched additional 'green' Australian Militia units to Port Moresby as the US 32nd and 41st Infantry Divisions arrived in Australia. The Australian Militia's 39th Battalion, already deployed at Port Moresby, was ordered north to defend Kokoda, which was attacked by the Japanese on 29 July. Eventually reinforced by Middle East veteran Australian Imperial Force (AIF) formations, the Australians combated IJA units across the Owen Stanley Range via the Kokoda Trail as the Japanese tried an over-land route to seize Port Moresby. By mid-September 1942, a stiffening Australian defence and orders for the Japanese advance to cease saved Port Moresby again. Also, a second amphibious Japanese invasion at Milne Bay during late August and early September 1942 aimed at seizing Port Moresby was turned back by Australian forces. Now, it was to become the American and Australians' turn to begin their offensive up the Kokoda Trail and through the jungle to drive the Japanese from Buna, Gona and Sanananda

On 10 September 1942, MacArthur ordered Lieutenant-General Robert L. Eichelberger's I Corps headquarters to deploy Major-General Edwin Harding's 32nd Infantry Division to capture the 11-mile-long group of Japanese installations at Buna. After a few months of arduous marching and combat against a bunkered Japanese foe, the unprepared American former National Guardsmen, with the aid of battle-hardened

---

ordered to seize Iwo Jima in the Volcano Islands south of the Bonin Island chain in February 1945. Iwo Jima is located in the Volcano Islands just to the south of the Bonin Island chain and to the Mariana Islands' north-west.

In the SPA, Vice-Admiral William Halsey commanded his Third Fleet up the Solomon Island chain with hellacious island combat in the New Georgia group (July–September 1943) and Bougainville (November 1943). From September–November 1944, Halsey's Third Fleet invaded and campaigned on Peleliu in the Palau Islands with the 1st Marine Division and the US Army's 81st Infantry Division.

In the SWPA, General Douglas MacArthur with his Australian and American ground forces and US Navy's Seventh Fleet vessels drove up the northern coast of North-east and Dutch New Guinea (1943–1944). The southern end of New Britain was invaded by Marine and US Army amphibious forces in December 1943, while Rabaul was neutralised in an aerial campaign, Operation *Cartwheel*.

After the conclusion of the brutal Peleliu campaign, the SPA and SWPA axes of advance converged for the invasion of Leyte in the Philippines in October 1944. (*Meridian Mapping*)

Australians, evicted the Japanese from their installations by January 1943. However, a steep Allied 'butcher bill' was incurred and MacArthur vowed, 'No more Bunas.'

After the bittersweet successes of Guadalcanal and Papua, three separate axes of Allied advances were conducted in the SWPA, South and Central Pacific areas. Beginning in January 1943, MacArthur's Australian-American forces seized strategic locales along the North-west New Guinea's northern coast and among nearby islands (e.g. Woodlark, Kiriwina, Goodenough) in the Solomon Sea as well as at the southern end of New Britain (Cape Gloucester and Arawe), while bypassing Japanese strongholds. Strategically, the Allies seized extant enemy or built new airfields for future operations and to neutralise Rabaul by air.

In the South Pacific Area (SPA), Admiral (promoted 18 November 1942) Halsey's forces of Marines and army troops quickly occupied and constructed airfields in the Russell Islands in late February 1943. Then the Solomon Island campaign continued with the invasion of the New Georgia group of islands in the Central Solomons in early July. After several weeks of combat against stubborn Japanese defenders, primarily centred on Munda Airfield, New Georgia Island fell as operations continued among other islands in the group: Arundel, Vella Lavella, Choiseul and the Treasuries.

These amphibious assaults served as a prelude to the invasion of the heavily defended and largest Solomon Island, Bougainville, along Cape Torokina at Empress Augusta Bay. On 1 November, I Marine Amphibious Corps (IMAC), initially commanded by Marine Lieutenant-General Vandegrift followed by Major-General Roy S. Geiger, comprised the 3rd Marine Division as well as Marine Raider and Defence Battalions. MacArthur wanted Halsey's aircraft established on new airfields at Cape Torokina within fighter-range of Rabaul in time to assist with the aerial neutralisation of that Japanese bastion as well as cover the 1st Marine Division's invasion of Cape Gloucester on 26 December.

Soon to follow IMAC was the US Army's XIV Corps (37th and Americal Divisions), under Major-General Oscar W. Griswold. XIV Corps enlarged and fortified the Cape Torokina perimeter, built new airfields, and awaited a massive IJA 17th Army counter-attack (to be launched in early March 1944), which was successfully defeated.

In the Central Pacific Area (CPA) of operations, under Admiral Chester W. Nimitz (also C-in-C, Pacific Ocean Area), the 2nd Marine Division along with elements of the US Army's 27th Division, comprising V Amphibious Corps (VAC, 35,000 troops), invaded the Gilbert Islands' Tarawa and Makin Atolls, respectively, the first major American offensive in this oceanic sector by the US Fifth Fleet, under the command of Vice-Admiral Raymond A. Spruance. After bloody combat from 20–23 November 1943 on mainly Betio Island in the south-west of Tarawa Atoll, against 4,500 suicidal, entrenched SNLF and Special Base Defence troops, the Gilbert group of islands and its airfields were seized at a steep price in American bloodshed (approximately

1,700 killed and 2,100 wounded). During the same time period, at Makin Atoll, principally on Butaritari Island, the 27th Division's 165th Infantry Regiment eliminated the small Japanese garrison's fortified positions one at a time. The USS *Liscome Bay*, an escort carrier, was sunk (644 sailors lost) by a Japanese submarine and the battleship USS *Mississippi* damaged with a turret fire (over forty seamen killed).

The Marshall Islands, a series of oceanic atolls, ceded to Japan at the end of the First World War, had numerous enemy airfields, sea-plane and naval bases dotted within the groups. Over 25,000 IJA and IJN troops awaited Nimitz's CPA move. Majuro Atoll (in the Marshall Islands' south-eastern sector) was initially occupied against limited enemy resistance by a reconnaissance company of Marines from VAC along with a battalion of the US 27th Division's 106th Infantry Regiment on 30 January 1944. The next day, the navy's Fifth Fleet (under Spruance) carrier aircraft attacked Japanese airfields on Kwajalein Atoll's islands. Roi-Namur Islands, the northernmost within Kwajalein Atoll, were attacked by the 4th Marine Division, while Kwajalein Island, at the atoll's south-eastern atoll tip, was invaded by the US 7th Infantry Division. Roi was secured on 1 February with Namur successfully occupied the next day. It was not until 4 February that Kwajalein Island was secured. The amphibious assault on Eniwetok Atoll began on 17 February with the separate 22nd Marines and elements of the US 27th Division's 106th Infantry Regiment attacking. The assault on Eniwetok Island's western landing beaches commenced on 19 February with the entire island secured two days later. Eniwetok Atoll's airfields and anchorages were to become the major staging areas for Nimitz's next CPA expedition, the Mariana Islands.

US Army and Marine forces invaded Saipan on 15 June 1944 and secured it after heavy fighting on 9 July. The IJN response to the US Fifth Fleet's presence resulted in the carrier aircraft clash on 19–20 June, the Battle of the Philippine Sea ('Great Marianas Turkey Shoot'), destroying IJN aerial capacity. Guam and Tinian, the other large islands in the Marianas, were invaded on 21 July and 24 July, respectively, and secured. Saipan and Tinian were to become major airbases for US B-29 bombing of Japan's Home Islands.

In September 1944, the islands of Peleliu and Angaur in the Palau group of the western Caroline Islands, directly due east of the large southern Philippine Island of Mindanao, were attacked primarily to secure the flank for MacArthur's return. The IJN bastion on Truk in the eastern Caroline Islands was bypassed. Of the two Palau islands, Peleliu with its airfield was the more important. In addition, Ulithi Atoll, to the north-east of the Palau group, was to be assaulted to obtain suitable anchorages for the massive US Navy fleet. Admiral Halsey, commander of the US Third Fleet, had reservations that an assault on the heavily defended Palaus was likely to be bloody. The Palaus had been reinforced with the IJA 14th Division, veterans from Manchuria, in mid-April 1944, augmenting this island group garrison's strength to 35,000 troops.

Nimitz had decided that the invasion of Peleliu was to be undertaken. However, Yap Atoll, situated between the Palau Islands and Ulithi Atoll, was to be bypassed.

Halsey's Third Fleet covered the landing of Geiger's III Amphibious Corps (IIIAC), comprising the 1st Marine Division (under Major-General William H. Rupertus, previously the Assistant Division Commander on Guadalcanal in 1942) and the Army's 81st Infantry Division's (under Major-General Paul J. Mueller), assaulting Peleliu on 15 September 1944. The Japanese mounted a suicidal defence of Peleliu from their complex of underground fortifications and strongpoints that emanated from the many natural caves on the Umurbrogel Ridges overlooking the airfield, just inland from the American assault beaches at the southern end of the island.

Intense combat ensued on Peleliu as the 1st Marine and army's 81st Divisions battled an enemy that preferred complete annihilation to surrender. Peleliu was not finally controlled until 27 November 1944. Over 25,000 other Japanese troops had been bypassed and isolated on the much larger northern Palau island of Babelthaup and other smaller nearby ones in the Palau groups. The 1st Marine Division lost 1,252 killed and 5,274 wounded or missing. The army's 81st Division lost 542 soldiers killed and 2,736 wounded. The total of nearly 10,000 American casualties, although numerically less than the approximately 14,000 Japanese troops killed, foreshadowed how the suicidal Japanese defensive paradigm was to delay the American advance on the island groups yet to be assaulted and exact steep casualties.

Elements of the US 81st Infantry Division attacked Angaur's smaller enemy garrison of 1,400 troops of a reinforced battalion of the IJA 59th Infantry Division on 17 September. Angaur was not completely neutralised until mid-October. Ulithi Atoll was seized by the US Army's XXIV Corps (under Major-General John R. Hodge) for future fleet anchorage.

The benefits of the Palau Islands victory have remained dubious. Mindanao and other southern Philippine Islands were bypassed by MacArthur in favour of a direct amphibious assault on Leyte. However, with this move by the SWPA force, the use of Angaur as a base for Japanese heavy bombers against a MacArthur-led Philippine Islands invasion was negated.

Throughout the earlier part of 1944, MacArthur's SWPA ground forces, comprising the US Sixth Army's (under Lieutenant-General Walter Krueger) 6th, 24th, 32nd and 41st Infantry Divisions, with attached elite cavalry, parachute, engineer and scout units, transported by the US Navy's growing amphibious fleet, had moved inexorably westward along the northern coast of Dutch New Guinea with successful missions at Saidor (2 January), the Admiralty Islands (29 February), Talasea (6 March), Aitape (22 April), Hollandia (22 April), Tanahmerah Bay (22 April), Wakde Island (18 May), Biak Island at the entrance of Geelvink Bay (27 May), Middelburg Island (30 June), Sansapor on the Vogelkop Peninsula (30 June), Noemfoor Island (2 July), and finally beyond New Guinea to Morotai Island in the Molucca chain of the Dutch East Indies (15 September).

Initially, at the Cairo conference of Allied war leaders in 1943, the ultimate aim of the American Pacific offensives was to be invasions of the Philippines, Formosa and the East China coast during late 1944 into the spring of 1945. Modifications arose and, in mid-1944, the American joints chiefs of staff instructed MacArthur's SWPA forces to liberate the Philippine Archipelago after focus had shifted away from an invasion of Formosa.

MacArthur's return to the Philippine Islands occurred with the massive invasion of Leyte by the US Sixth Army on 20 October 1944 after US Ranger assaults on smaller islands in Leyte Gulf. General Tomoyuki Yamashita, the 'Tiger of Malaya', was the Japanese military governor of the Philippines from September 1944. Additionally, he commanded the IJA Fourteenth Army headquartered in Manila on 10 October. The US Sixth Army landed along Leyte's assault beaches with the transport and protection of Halsey's Third Fleet and Vice-Admiral Thomas Kinkaid's Seventh Fleet, where the latter served as MacArthur's commander for the Allied Naval Forces in SWPA. With tough enemy ground resistance to the Sixth Army's X and XXIV Corps on Leyte, the IJN launched the Battle of Leyte Gulf on 25 October, which Kinkaid's offshore Seventh Fleet survived. From the end of October until mid-December, the US 7th, 24th, 32nd, 77th and 96th Infantry Divisions, among other formations, made slow but steady progress against a number of IJA defensive ridge and valley positions. MacArthur announced an end to major combat operations on Leyte on 25 December.

The final liberation campaign for the Philippine Islands started with the invasion of Luzon at Lingayen Gulf by the Sixth Army's I and XIV Corps, the US X and XXIV Corps having remained on Leyte. MacArthur also had the US Eighth Army (under Eichelberger), comprising the 1st Cavalry, 11th Airborne, 24th, 32nd and 38th Infantry Divisions as well as an independent 112th Cavalry Regiment, as a strategic reserve. Bataan (16 February), Corregidor (2 March) and Manila (4 March) were all reclaimed by MacArthur's forces, although it was not to be until 5 July that the SWPA commander announced the final liberation of the Philippines. The capture of the Philippines enabled the Allies to construct newer plans for the invasion of the Japanese Home Islands.

After the capture of the Marianas, Nimitz was ordered to seize enemy-held islands in the Bonin, Volcano and Ryukyu Islands. Iwo Jima, located in the Volcano Islands, just to the south of the Bonin Island chain, to Japan's south-east and north-west of the Marianas, was to be invaded one month after the MacArthur Luzon landings.

Iwo Jima was heavily fortified and the site of two well-constructed air bases, which enabled Japan to base their fighter squadrons to interdict the westward American advance across the Central Pacific Ocean towards the East China Sea. Also, the Iwo

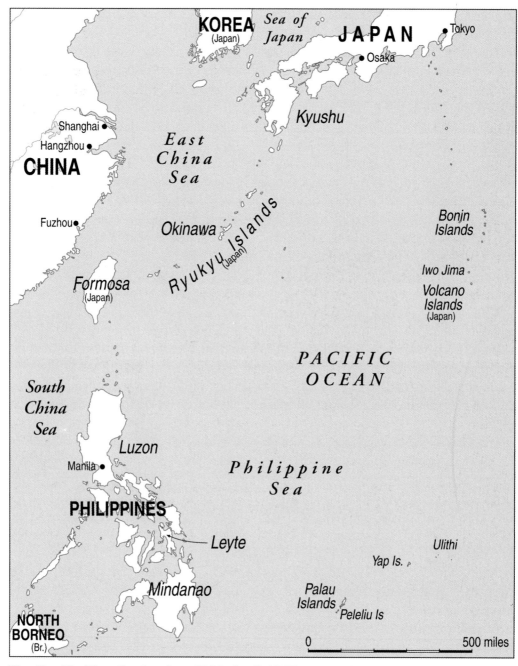

The Pacific War, September 1944–April 1945. In mid-1944, MacArthur's SWPA ground and naval forces were ordered to liberate the Philippines beginning in October 1944 at Leyte, rather than invade Formosa further north and closer to Japan's Home Islands.

To secure MacArthur's eastern flank at Leyte, Halsey's SPA Third Fleet attacked Peleliu in the Palau group of the western Caroline Islands, directly due east of Mindanao, in September.

Jima airfields were ideal for American light bombers attacking the Japanese homeland, P-51 fighter escorts to accompany the Mariana-based B-29 bombers, and emergency landing fields for damaged Superfortresses that were suffering heavy losses on their 2,500-mile round-trip from Tinian and Saipan to bomb Japanese cities and military installations. Allied planners also believed that American occupation of Iwo Jima would deal a psychological blow to Japanese morale as the island was traditionally viewed as Nipponese territory administered from Tokyo. For these reasons, the US Marine Corps was to embark on one of its most bitter campaigns during the war in the Pacific.

On 19 February 1945, the 4th and 5th Marine Divisions arrived off Iwo Jima to commence the island's amphibious assault. Ultimately, the 3rd Marine Division was employed for the island's capture. After bloody combat amid the volcanic ash of the beach-head and the entrenched Japanese positions, especially at Mount Suribachi, the

---

Leyte was invaded by the Sixth Army's X and XXIV Corps on 20 October with the transport and protection of Admiral Halsey's Third and Kinkaid's Seventh Fleets. MacArthur declared major combat operations on Leyte completed on 25 December.

The final liberation campaign for the Philippines started with the invasion of Luzon at Lingayen Gulf by the Sixth Army's I and XIV Corps on 9 January 1945. Bataan (16 February), Corregidor (2 March), and Manila (4 March) were all reclaimed by MacArthur's forces, although it was not to be until 5 July that the SWPA commander announced the Philippines' final liberation.

After the seizure of the Marianas, Nimitz was ordered to seize Iwo Jima, located in the Volcano Islands just to the south of the Bonin Island chain and to Japan's south-east and the Mariana Islands' north-west. Iwo Jima was invaded in February 1945, one month after the MacArthur Luzon landings.

Iwo Jima was a heavily fortified island with two well-constructed air bases, which enabled Japanese fighter squadrons to interdict the advancing American LOC further westward across the CPA towards the East China Sea. Once captured, these airfields could base P-51 fighter escorts to accompany the Mariana-based B-29 bombers that were suffering heavy losses on their 2,500-mile round trip over Japanese cities and military targets. On 19 February, the 4th and 5th Marine Divisions of Spruance's Fifth Fleet and Central Pacific Task Forces, commenced the island's amphibious assault. Ultimately, the 3rd Marine Division was employed for the island's capture. By 7 April, the P-51 fighters were able to fly escort for the B-29s. Also, Iwo Jima provided emergency landing fields for damaged Superfortresses beginning on 4 March.

Following the Philippines' liberation and Iwo Jima's capture; ground forces from SWPA were to combine with Spruance's Fifth Fleet and Central Pacific Task Forces for the invasion of the Ryukyu Islands, an archipelago of three island groups (gunto), totalling 161 islands. The Ryukyus, extending from Japan's southern Home Island of Kyushu to Formosa's north-eastern end, served as a tactical barrier to an Allied advance from the Pacific Ocean towards the Asian mainland, Korea and the western coast of Japan as this island chain served as the eastern boundary of the East China Sea The Okinawa gunto is in between the Amami Islands to the north and the Sakishima ones to the south. Okinawa is the largest island in the Ryukyus, being situated only 325 miles south-west of Kyushu and was the most heavily fortified. As the Iwo Jima landings were delayed until 19 February, the Tenth Army's invasion of Okinawa was postponed until 1 April, to allow for arrival of surface fleet and carrier air support of the amphibious landings. (Meridian Mapping)

4th and 5th Marine Divisions disembarked on 19 and 26 March, respectively. By 7 April, the P-51 fighters were able to fly from Iwo Jima for escort missions for the B-29 attacks on Japan. The cost in American bloodshed to seize such a small island over a month of hellacious combat was staggering. The total number of Marines and US Navy sailors killed was 6,821, with an additional 21,865 other casualties. When the war had ended a total of 24,761 American airmen were rescued when 2,251 B-29s made emergency landings at Iwo Jima. In fact, the initial B-29 emergency landing on Iwo Jima was on 4 March. If not for the valiant Marines' sacrifice to capture the island, many of those airmen would have died. For their gallantry, twenty-seven Congressional Medals of Honor, the largest number won by Marines and sailors in one single battle, were awarded.

Following the Philippines' liberation and Iwo Jima's seizure, the SWPA and CPA theatres of operations were to converge on the Ryukyu Islands for a planned 1 March 1945 invasion, to obtain suitable Allied staging areas and airfields for the all-out invasion of Japan's Home Islands. However, due to a delayed start of the Iwo Jima landings (not until 19 February), Operation Iceberg, the invasion of Okinawa, was postponed until 1 April to allow the Allied surface fleet and carrier air support to cover the amphibious landings. Okinawa was to become Nimitz's main target and this island's invasion was to become the biggest and costliest operation of the war.

In early 1945, the Imperial High Command had decided that the final decisive battle of the war was to be fought in the Home Islands. However, the main defensive effort was to first occur in the Ryukyus' area. When it was clear that the Americans were committed to Okinawa's capture, conserved Japanese air strength for *kamikaze* attacks and special surface 'suicide attack boats' were intended to wreak havoc on the Allied invasion fleet. The IJA's 32nd Army's tenacious and suicidal defence of Okinawa on the ground was to simply be a delaying action.

(**Opposite, above**) A B-25B medium Mitchell bomber takes off from the USS *Hornet* to commence Lieutenant-Colonel James H. Doolittle's 'Tokyo Raid'. US Navy Captain Marc A. Mitscher commanded the *Hornet's* maiden voyage. Vice-Admiral Halsey commanded Task Force (TF)-16, comprising the *Hornet* and USS *Enterprise* as well as escorting cruisers and destroyers. At 0820hrs on 18 April 1942 amid rough seas, sixteen B-25Bs from the 17th Bombardment Group launched earlier than planned after TF-16 was sighted by an enemy picket vessel. Admiral Isoroku Yamamoto, commander of the IJN's Combined Fleet, and other IJN commanders were humiliated by the 'Doolittle Raid's' propaganda coup heralding the start of an American counter-offensive in the Pacific. The 'Tokyo Raid' contributed to the Japanese military leaders' support for a Midway Island invasion for June. (*NARA*)

(**Opposite, below**) Four Marines carry a wounded rifleman on a litter along a battle-scarred, frond-littered path through a coconut grove during a Matanikau River battle on Guadalcanal in late October 1942. The area around the river's mouth was a hotbed of action since September. The defence of Henderson Field and final eviction of the Japanese from this southern Solomon island lasted from 7 August until 9 February 1943, constituting the first American ground counter-offensive victory in the SPA. (*NARA*)

"HORNET"

(**Above**) Marines douse a Grumman F4F Wildcat's smoking engine near a hangar on Guadalcanal's Henderson Field, an 'unsinkable aircraft carrier'. Note some of the Marines were wearing sidearms, while the Marine to the right of the Wildcat's propeller wore a First World War and interwar-years steel helmet that the US had adapted from the British 'Brodie' helmet. Henderson Field was constantly besieged by IJA infiltration and ground attacks, frequent enemy air-raids and intermittent IJN surface ship bombardment during the six-month campaign. (*NARA*)

(**Opposite, above**) A beached Japanese landing barge or Daihatsu near Kokumbona (on Guadalcanal's northern coast) after American air attack. Marine Dauntless SBD dive-bombers and army P-400 fighter-bombers were especially effective at interdicting Japanese re-supply and reinforcement traffic. Each barge carried seventy troops or 12 tons of cargo or a medium tank and had a bow hull ramp that lowered into the sand to deliver its load directly to the shore. Ironically, Marine Lieutenant Victor H. Krulak's (who was to be a staff officer of the 6th Marine Division on Okinawa) observed these crafts' bow ramp design in China. With Andrew Higgins' boat yards and Krulak's notes, the US Navy was to utilise similarly designed landing craft ('Higgins boats') to deliver assault waves, vehicles, supplies and reinforcements to hostile shores throughout the entire Pacific War. (*NARA*)

(**Opposite, below**) Australian militia and native carriers stop at Eora Creek Village on 1 September 1942 during their retreat from a forward area along the Kokoda Trail as the Japanese drove southward from Buna over the Owen Stanley Range to seize Port Moresby. A planned Japanese amphibious assault on Port Moresby was thwarted with the IJN's strategic defeat at the Battle of the Coral Sea in early May 1942 as well as in late August to early September, when Australian forces repelled a Japanese amphibious landing at Milne Bay, on the eastern tip of Papua. (*NARA*)

(**Above**) Australian militiamen gaze with binoculars and a telescope at the enemy across a valley in the Owen Stanley Range near Uberti to the south of Ioribaiwa along the Imita Ridge in mid-September 1942. The Japanese over-land offensive, which had pushed the Australians southward with their advance towards Port Moresby, had shifted to the defensive on Imperial High Command orders after repeated IJA attempts to vanquish the 1st Marine Division on Guadalcanal failed. Reinforcements destined for Papua were instead shifted to Guadalcanal. The AIF's 25th Brigade of Middle East combat veterans was to launch its attack against Japanese positions along the Imita Ridge on 26 September. (*NARA*)

(**Opposite, above**) Australian infantry behind an Australian-crewed M3 'Stuart' light tank advance with limited cover from the Giropi Plantations coconut trees near Buna. A Bren gunner (*right of the tank*) fire his LMG from the hip directly at the Japanese pillbox (*background*). MacArthur's northern Papuan offensive had started with the Australians' movement up the Kokoda Trail at the end of September 1942 and was followed by the deployment of the US 32nd Infantry Division's battalions in November 1942. The reduction of the Japanese garrison at Buna, 'Bloody Buna', required direct gunfire from the tank's 37mm turret ordnance to overcome a suicidal enemy defence from their bunkered positions. (*NARA*)

(**Opposite, below**) Across a waterway from Buna Mission, a 37mm AT gun-crew of the 128th US Infantry Regiment, 32nd Division, fires at Japanese pillboxes halting the Allied advance to recapture northern Papua, in late autumn 1942. The earthen and log-fortified Japanese bunkers required artillery, aerial attack, direct tank gunfire and TNT satchels to destroy them. Allied casualties were exorbitantly high convincing MacArthur of 'No More Bunas'. (*NARA*)

(**Above**) Approaching Munda Airfield near New Georgia's Blanche Channel (*background*), an Army XIV Corps flame-thrower unit sends a plume of flame at a Japanese pillbox delaying the airstrip's seizure in early August 1943. Two soldiers provide suppressive rifle fire against the pillbox and any dug-in enemy infantry in rifle pits that had refused to surrender. (*NARA*)

(**Opposite, above**) A Japanese soldier lies dead after shooting himself with his *Arisaka* rifle by using his toe near Munda Airfield on New Georgia in August 1943. By so doing, he prevented capture with its attendant dishonour to his warrior (*bushido*) code. Choosing death over capture was to become a ubiquitous scene at all combat locales in the Pacific. (*NARA*) *GOOD!*

(**Opposite, below**) A Marine Chance-Vought F4U-1 Corsair takes off from battle-scarred Munda Airfield in late summer 1943. The Corsair, with it inverted gull-wing design, was planned as a carrie borne fighter for the US Navy. However, as both carrier landing problems and ground combat success demonstrated, it became an excellent land-based ground-attack and close-support fighter-bomber, which fulfilled Marine aviation doctrine to assist the Corps' rifle platoons to reach their objective with a minimum of casualties. The Corsair entered operational service in 1943. (*NARA*)

A US paratrooper from a battalion of the 503rd Parachute Infantry Regiment (PIR) shakes hands with an Australian infantryman holding his Owen SMG, manufactured in Port Kemba and Newcastle. The American paratroopers had jumped at low altitude, amid a smoke-screen and a large fighter and bomber protective umbrella, onto a landing field at Nadzab, approximately 30 miles west of Lae, on 5 September 1943. Meeting no opposition, the paratroopers seized the drop-zone to airlift in the Australian 7th Division within forty-eight hours. The combined air, sea and inland assaults cut off the Japanese 51st Division at Lae from General Adachi's 18th Army forces. (*NARA*)

(**Opposite, above**) Australian gunners man a 40mm Bofors gun at Lae Village in anticipation of a Japanese air strike after that locale at the eastern base of the Huon Peninsula was captured in September 1943. Prompt protection of captured airfields and other strategic bases was a necessity in the Pacific campaign, as the Japanese were quick to launch aerial counter-attacks. (*NARA*)

(**Opposite, below**) An Australian soldier carries a wounded mate behind a Matilda Infantry tank near the village of Sattleberg on the Huon Peninsula during the trek to capture Finschhafen. The Japanese could not linger for long in the inhospitable mountain terrain beyond the Markham and Ramu river valleys, nor could the Allies leave such a large enemy pocket as Finschhafen in enemy hands. On 22 September 1943, Admiral Barbey's US Seventh Amphibious Fleet deposited the AIF's 20th Brigade to begin their assault on Finschhafen. (*NARA*)

A list of the campaigns fought by the US Sixth Army is shown on a tent wall at Lieutenant-General Walter Krueger's headquarters. *(USAMHI)*

American soldiers of the most combat-experienced 163rd RCT, 41st Division as well as the 127th RCT, 32nd Division, both having been refitted in Australia by Eichelberger's I Corps after the Papuan campaign, land on Aitape Beach on 22 April 1944. The three closest soldiers are armed with the M1 carbine, which was a more compact weapon than the M1 Garand for jungle operations. It was gas-operated and semi-automatic like the M1 Garand rifle but weighed 4lb less even though it had a 15- or 30-round detachable box magazine. (NARA)

Soldiers of the 163rd RCT, 41st Division search for cover on the beach of Wakde Island after landing there on 18 May 1944. In the background is the LCVP that unloaded the soldiers at the shoreline. The previous day, elements of this formation landed unopposed in Maffin Bay near Sarmi. Wakde Island proved to be a much more difficult mission. It took two days of close fighting to wrest the roughly 800 Japanese troops from their 'spider holes', coconut log bunkers and caves. (NARA)

(**Above**) An American soldier in chest-high water crossing a stream in Hollandia using a rope-anchored native canoe. Hollandia, on the northern coast of Dutch New Guinea, was another SWPA invasion site on 22 April 1944 to seize vital airfields. The Hollandia operation was coupled with simultaneous assaults at Aitape and Tanamerah Bay to dominate a 150-mile stretch of coastline, which would entrap roughly 60,000 Japanese bypassed troops. (*NARA*)

(**Opposite, above**) An LCM unloads both 24th Infantry Division soldiers and an M8 HMC at Tanahmerah Bay on 22 April 1944. A rapid advance was expected. However, congestion and a re-supply problem ensued as it was very difficult to move vehicles off the dense beach sand. The 24th Division infantrymen advanced slowly having to hand-carry all their supplies and living for weeks on half rations. (*NARA*)

(**Opposite, below**) A P-38 Lightning comes to rest after landing at Korako Airstrip at Aitape on the north coast of New Guinea in the late spring of 1944. The P-38 was a heavy fighter that carried two booms supporting the main units of the tricycle landing gear as well as the two engines' turbochargers. With a maximum speed of more than 400mph, a range of 2,600 miles along with its nose armament of a 20mm cannon and four 0.5-inch fixed forward-firing machine-guns, this plane immensely contributed to the Allies gaining fighter aerial superiority in the SWPA. The P-38 carried an external bomb or rocket load of two tons, making it a powerful fighter-bomber too. (*NARA*)

The fighter strip at Cape Torokina's shoreline in late 1944, seen from an aircraft flying over it. Eight US Navy construction battalions ('Seabees') and one New Zealand engineer brigade began work on the strip at a relatively dry area along the edge of Cape Torokina in Empress Augusta Bay on 10 November 1943. Remarkably, the fighter strip was ready for operation on 10 December, when Marine Chance-Vought F4U-1 Corsairs flew into their new base. (*NARA*)

(**Opposite, above**) Two 3rd Division Marines on the northern Solomon island of Bougainville in an improvised emplacement made with a tent half-sheet roof and a log embrasure to house their M1917A1 0.30-inch calibre Browning water-cooled medium machine-gun with a muzzle flash suppressor. Such positions were established to guard trails where the enemy was expected to come down onto the Torokina beach-head from the hilly surrounding inland region in November 1943. (*NARA*)

(**Opposite, below**) Soldiers of Company A, 145th Infantry Regiment, 37th Division man a M1917A1 0.30-inch-calibre medium machine-gun position as part of the army's XIV Corps perimeter on 10 March 1944. General Hyakutake, the 17th Army commander on Bougainville, counter-attacked the XIV Corps perimeter in early March 1944. The Japanese still believed at this late date that if the XIV Corps perimeter was breached with the capture of the three Allied airfields at Torokina, then Rabaul's aerial neutralisation could be interrupted allowing that enemy northern New Britain Island bastion to resume its integral role in the SPA and SWPA. Hyakutake amassed over 15,000 infantry and artillery troops, the latter manning 75mm-pack Howitzers, 105mm and 150mm guns, which were hauled onto ridges dominating the perimeter, to hurl against the American perimeter. This March 1944 counter-offensive was the greatest concentration of IJA forces that would fight in the SPA and could have been larger. However, Hyakutake retained the 17th Army's remaining 18,000 troops to man the Buka and Buin garrisons at Bougainville's northern and southern ends, respectively. (*NARA*)

2nd Division Marines take cover from enemy fire and man a 0.30-inch calibre LMG behind a Betio Island demolished sea-wall in Tarawa Atoll. The Marines and some attached US Army 27th Division infantrymen assaulted the Gilbert Islands from 20–23 November 1943, paying a steep price in bloodshed – 3,200 Marine casualties – against fanatic Japanese SNLF and Special Base Defence Force troops. This initial US offensive in the CPA ominously presaged suicidal enemy defences at the landing beaches. Only one Japanese officer and sixteen enlisted men surrendered from a garrison of over 3,500 at Tarawa. (NARA)

Marines use the protection of the Burns Phillips Pier to get ashore at Red Beach on 20 November 1943 on Tarawa Atoll's Betio Island in the Gilbert Islands. Due to a low tide, even shallow-draft Higgins boats transporting the 2nd Marine Division's assault wave were unable to clear the reef, leaving riflemen as far as 500 yards from shore. As amphibious tracked vehicles were utilised to clear the reef to get onto the assault beaches, they were set ablaze by Japanese gunfire from fortified bunkers near the water's edge. (NARA)

A Marine fires on a Japanese fortified mound of sand, earth and coral (*background*). Many of these pillboxes were strengthened with coconut logs to withstand naval and aerial bombardment. American light and medium tanks along with Marine flame-thrower and demolitions teams were required to reduce the Japanese bunkers. (*NARA*)

(**Above**) Soldiers of the US 7th Infantry Division attack a Japanese pillbox with a flame-thrower on Kwajalein Island in the Japanese-mandated Marshall Islands' Kwajalein Atoll during operations from 29 January–3 February 1944. The 4th Marine Division amphibiously assaulted two other of the atoll's northern islands, Roi-Namur. The Marshall Islands' capture yielded extant airfields to the US Navy and represented American penetration of Japan's 'outer ring' of defences in the CPA. (*NARA*)

(**Opposite, above**) A contingent of the 22nd Marines as well as assorted shallow-draft and armoured tracked vessels are seen ashore on one of Eniwetok Atoll's islands in the Marshalls' group from 17–21 February 1944. The US Army's 106th Infantry Regiment of the 27th Division also fought among Eniwetok Atoll's islands. The Japanese learned that their shoreline fortifications were too vulnerable to US naval and aerial bombardment, so in future tactics the enemy shifted to prepared defences in depth on their other island possessions. (*NARA*)

(**Opposite, below**) Two Marines on Saipan search a cave for hiding Japanese soldiers. Both Marines aim hand-guns at the mouth of the cave, the one on the left holding his venerable 1911 0.45-inch calibre semi-automatic pistol. Saipan, in the Mariana Islands, was invaded on 15 June 1944 and was not secured until 9 July with the US 2nd Marine and the US 27th Infantry Divisions having successfully defeated the IJA 43rd Division. Successful American invasions of other large islands in the Mariana Group, Guam and Tinian, followed. The Marianas' seizure shortened the range for American B-29 bombers to 1,300 miles from Japan's Home Islands. The Superfortresses also regularly attacked Japanese installations in the Philippines for MacArthur's upcoming invasion. Japanese air attacks, principally launched from Iwo Jima, against the newly operational American bomber aerodromes, were a predictable enemy response to the Marianas' conquest. (*NARA*)

(**Above**) A 2nd Division Marine gazes at Japanese civilians who jumped off a cliff into the rock-strewn waters below rather than surrender. Some 1,000 Japanese civilians on Saipan committed suicide during the last days of the battle. Many jumped from seaside heights that were later known as 'Suicide' and '*Banzai*' cliffs. (*NARA*)

(**Opposite, above**) The 1st Division's 7th Marines take cover from an intense Japanese mortar and artillery barrage at Orange Beach 3's shoreline at the extreme right of the Peleliu's assault beaches in the Palau Group on 15 September 1944. Capsized and smoking remains of Marine amphibious tractors are seen near the water's edge and along a pier (*background*), precluding timely re-supply, reinforcements and wounded evacuation. Horrific combat raged on Peleliu against the IJA 14th Division until November 1944. Peleliu's invasion by the 1st Marine, and later the US Army's 81st Infantry Divisions, was strategically justified to secure the island's enemy airfield to protect the US Sixth Army's flank during the upcoming Leyte invasion. The cost of Peleliu's seizure resulted in over 2,300 Americans killed and almost 8,500 wounded. (*NARA*)

(**Opposite, below**) A 37mm AT gun manned by 1st Division Marines fires against Japanese gun and troop positions housed in concrete structures near Peleliu's airfield, where the 1st, 5th and 7th Marines landed on 15 September 1944. The Japanese had constructed strongpoints at the shoreline and inland, from rough coral and boulders, in addition to concrete structures (*background*). The next day, the 5th Marines moved onto the cratered airfield, starting a day-long melee against Japanese entrenchments. Eventually, the US 81st Infantry Division assisted the Marines after its 17 September Angaur Island (to Peleliu's south-west) invasion was completed within a few days. (*NARA*)

(**Above**) Sprawled and charred Japanese tank crewmen next to their destroyed A-Type 95 (*Ke-Go*) light tank near Peleliu's airfield on 16 September 1944. The Type 95 light tank was thinly armoured and had one 37mm turret gun and two 7.7mm rear turret and hull machine-guns. They were no match for the few Marine M4 medium tanks that eventually were able to land and move inland toward the airfield to assist the Marine riflemen on D-Day+1. *(NARA)*

(**Opposite, above**) The initial US Sixth Army's X and XXIV Corps landing's assault wave lands on Leyte on 20 October 1944. The amphibious operations centred on Tacloban, Dulag and the Panaon Strait. Three days earlier, US Army Rangers from the 6th Battalion seized Suluan and Dingat Islands in Leyte Gulf. MacArthur's invasion forces faced the IJA 16th Division and assorted support units, numbering 21,000 troops. *(NARA)*

(**Opposite, below**) The vast American naval armada comprising Admiral Halsey's Third Fleet, with TF-38 of four fast carrier task groups, along with Vice-Admiral Kinkaid's Seventh Fleet supports the US Sixth Army's X and XXIV Corps at Leyte Gulf on 20 October 1944. Naval airpower and gunfire were needed to both defend the fleet and provide firepower for MacArthur's troops ashore until working airfields were seized and refurbished, as Lieutenant-General George C. Kenney's Fifth Air Force based on Morotai did not have the range for its land-based fighters to provide this support. US Navy forces also had the responsibility of interdicting any IJA reinforcements to Leyte from Luzon and from other garrisons in the Philippines. *(NARA)*

(**Opposite, above**) American infantrymen trek through a Leyte swamp on 3 November 1944 with the support of an LVT (A)-4 ('Amtracs'), which was designed for operation in such areas inaccessible to wheeled vehicles or boats. The LVT (A)-1 initially had a 37mm turret gun. However, this provided limited firepower so a 75mm M2/M3 Howitzer was installed mounted in the turret of the M8 HMC and designated the LVT (A)-4 with a crew of six. At Leyte, there were over ten 'Amtrac' battalions in the US Sixth Army. (*NARA*)

(**Above**) A kit-laden US Army M8 HMC fires a 75mm round at a Japanese bunker on Leyte several weeks after the initial invasion. These armoured vehicles were typically assigned to Reconnaissance Squadrons in order to provide close support against enemy fortified positions. The high degree of elevation that could be achieved by the turret's Howitzer (40 degrees) enabled it to reduce Japanese troops and gun emplacements that were bunkered on the sides of hills. (*NARA*)

(**Opposite, below**) US Sixth Army infantrymen clear out a Leyte village on 31 October 1944. The soldiers are assisted by an M4 medium tank with its 75mm turret gun and a LVT-2 (Buffalo), the latter armed with 0.50-inch calibre heavy machine-guns used primarily for troop and cargo transport. (*NARA*)

(**Above**) American soldiers fire their 57mm AT gun against Japanese positions in the Cabusilan Hills, the most prominent section of the Zambales Mountains, the latter separating Luzon's central plain from the South China Sea, approximately 5 miles from Clark Field in early February 1945. MacArthur directed Krueger to recapture Clark Field, on 17 January 1945, but logistics delayed the advance towards the aerodrome until 21 January. Elements from XIV Corps' 37th and 40th Infantry Divisions initiated their attacks on 27–28 January. Clark Field was valued as a base for close air support as it possessed several airfields. It was principally defended by the Japanese *Kembu* Group's several thousand troops, who were also positioned across the eastern approaches of the Zambales Mountains overlooking the runways. (*NARA*)

(**Opposite, above**) American soldiers take cover behind an M4 medium tank during the advance towards Manila in early February 1945. Manila, the capital of the Philippines located in southern Luzon across Manila Bay from the Bataan Peninsula, had 1 million inhabitants. Having largely escaped destruction in 1942 when MacArthur declared it an 'open city', it became a major urban battleground as the SWPA commander was determined to recapture it. (*NARA*)

(**Opposite, below**) An 81mm M1 mortar crew of the US 32nd Division, veterans of Buna and the New Guinea campaign, crouches as a Japanese shell has exploded nearby in the Cagayan Valley in the northern portion of Philippine island of Luzon in April 1945. The US Sixth Army comprising I and XIV Corps (with accompanying elite Ranger, Scout and Engineer units) landed at Luzon's Lingayen Gulf on 9 January. The 32nd Division was sent to reinforce I Corps (initially comprising the 6th and 43rd Infantry Divisions) in late January to support the move onto Manila, which fell to the American troops on 4 March. The US Army's 25th and 32nd Infantry Divisions' advance into the Cagayan Valley, via Santa Fe, was slowed by both steep mountainous terrain of northern Luzon and Japanese defences. (*NARA*)

(**Above**) A US Sixth Army's 25th Infantry Division soldier aims his bazooka for firing on the enemy on a hillside in an attempt to seize the Balete Pass, the key route situated between San Jose and Santa Fe, to reach Baguio, the summer capital from where General Tomoyuki Yamashita directed the stubborn Japanese defence along northern Luzon's mountainous region during April 1945. The 25th Division comprised veterans of Guadalcanal and the New Georgia campaign. Northern Luzon was Yamashita's last major redoubt, manned by more than 150,000 Japanese soldiers concentrated near Baguio. (NARA)

(**Opposite, above**) An LVT 1 (Alligator) carries elements of the 4th Marine Division towards the assault beaches of Iwo Jima at 0830hrs on 19 February 1945. The 3rd and 5th Marine Divisions of the VAC were also employed in the invasion of this Volcano Island, 750 miles south of Tokyo. A US Navy battleship, the USS *Idaho*, takes up her bombardment station against Japanese positions near Mount Suribachi (*background*), the island's highest point at 528 feet, situated in the extreme south-western sector. (NARA)

(**Opposite, below**) Three Marines drag a cart from one of their LCVP vessels with its bow ramp lowered at the water's edge while under enemy fire. The Japanese defenders, built around the IJA 109th Division, employed inland entrenched guns as heavy as 150mm against the assault waves approaching the shoreline. The dense network of hidden artillery positions was secluded in more than 11 miles of underground tunnels, some situated behind reinforced steel doors within Mount Suribachi. The Marines stormed ashore at Green, Red 1 and 2, Yellow 1 and 2, and Blue 1 and 2 Beaches on 19 February 1945 along the south-eastern shore of the island between Mount Suribachi to the south-west and the East Boat Basin to the north-east. Airfield Number 1 was located directly inland from the Marine assault beaches. (NARA)

(**Opposite, above**) While some Marines were pinned down by Japanese mortar, rocket and artillery fire on Red Beach on 19 February 1945, others attempted to move inland onto terrace slopes of volcanic ash as high as 15-feet. After hitting the beach, many Marines sank ankle deep into the soft ash, which slowed their pace carrying kit and equipment often weighing between 50 to 120lb. The Japanese defenders had no immediate fortifications on the landing beaches to resist the Marines as it was intended to draw them onto the Motoyama Plain, where gunfire from well-prepared underground positions were to wreak havoc against the invaders. Enemy fire erupted just over an hour after the Marines crowded ashore on the landing beaches with machine-guns, mortars and heavy artillery. (*NARA*)

(**Above**) Six Marines manhandle a 37mm M3A1 AT gun along a rough inland path on 1 March 1945. Although antiquated by this stage of the war, the 37mm gun still had value in the Pacific campaign as it did not require towing and could be rapidly re-positioned over rough ground with its relative light weight. Once positioned, the 37mm AT gun was capable of firing AP, HE rounds against Japanese light/medium tanks, entrenched pillboxes and caves. (*NARA*)

(**Opposite, below**) Marine riflemen use large rocks for cover while a flame-thrower team applies its incendiary liquid into a cave that sequestered suicidal Japanese defenders on Iwo Jima. It was estimated that a few thousand Japanese remained hidden in caves and underground tunnels after the island was deemed 'secure'. (*NARA*)

One of the most iconic images of the Pacific campaign, taken by Joe Rosenthal, an Associated Press photographer, depicted six Marines from Company E, 2nd Battalion, 28th Marines, raising the 'Stars and Stripes' atop Mount Suribachi on 23 February 1945. Three of the six Marines shown were subsequently killed in action. This photograph became the imagery basis for the Marine Corps War (Iwo Jima) Memorial located near Arlington National Cemetery and the Marine Corps Museum at Quantico, both in Virginia. *(NARA)*

A P-51 Mustang fighter takes off from the 6,400ft-long runway of the re-built Airfield 1 with Mount Suribachi in the background. The fighters were now able to escort B-29 bombers on their Mariana Islands-based missions over the Japanese Home Islands. The rebuilt enemy airfields were also able to serve as emergency landing strips for the Superfortresses, saving thousands of American airmen from loss at sea on the return trip to Saipan and Tinian. (NARA)

Chapter Two

Terrain, Fortifications and Weapons

The 161 Ryukyu Islands, divided into three major groups (*gunto*), serve as the East China Sea's eastern boundary from Kyushu (southern Japanese Home Island) to Formosa's north-eastern end. From north-to-south are Amami, Okinawa and Sakishima *Guntos*. The Ryukyus formed a barrier to Allied advances towards the Asian mainland, Korea and Japan's western coast. Okinawa, the most heavily defended and largest island (60 miles long) in the Okinawa *Gunto*, was targeted for invasion as it was only 325 miles south-west of Kyushu, Japan, with ample suitable ground for airfields. Yontan and Kadena airfields on the island's western coast served as major factors for the US Tenth Army's assault landings there. On the eastern side of Okinawa's Katchin Peninsula, Chimu Bay and Nakagusuku (later Buckner Bay) were identified as the only two substantial fleet anchorages between Kyushu and Formosa for staging a Home Islands invasion.

To Okinawa's west were Kerama Retto, Ie Shima, Kume Shima and Aguni Shima, with the initial two becoming adjuncts to Operation *Iceberg*. A group of islands, called the Eastern Islands (reconnoitred by elements of the US 27th Infantry Division) paralleled Okinawa's east central coast. Kerama Retto was 15 miles from Okinawa, while Ie Shima and the Eastern Islands were 10 miles away.

Okinawa is irregularly shaped, orientated north-east to south-west, and widest (18 miles) where the Motobu Peninsula extends into the East China Sea. Okinawa's narrowest point, Ishikawa Isthmus (2 miles) near Chimu Bay, divides the island into two contrasting regions. To the north the terrain is dominated by heavily wooded and mountainous country. To the south a valley running from Naha, the prefectural capital on the western coast, to Yonabarua on the east coast to the north of the Chinen Peninsula consists of steep cliffs, deep ravines and hills. Okinawa's triangle-shaped southernmost third is dotted with hills and some vast 500-foot-high ridges, made chiefly of limestone and 'honeycombed' by underground streams. Several escarpments and ridges provided the Japanese with successive defensive lines against an American southward drive. The Oroku Peninsula is situated on the west coast just south of the city of Naha.

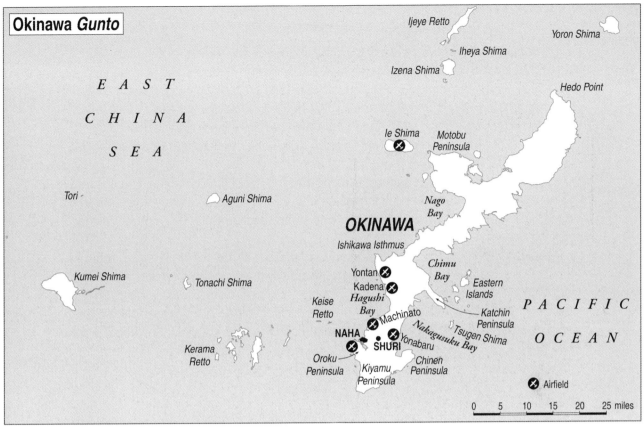

Okinawa and surrounding islands. The irregularly shaped, 60-mile-long island of Okinawa, replete with airfields (Yontan, Kadena, Machinato, Yonabaru and Naha), became the Allied strategic target for a massive amphibious assault as a stepping-stone for the invasion of Japan. To Okinawa's west were Kerama Retto, Ie Shima (with two airfields), Kumei Shima and Aguni Shima. Kerama Retto (15 miles from Okinawa) and Ie Shima were also to be assaulted as part of the invasion's plan, while the more proximate Keise Retto, the Eastern Islands and Tsugen Shima were to be reconnoitred or seized.

The Japanese airfields at Yontan and Kadena on the island's western coast served as a major factor for the Tenth Army's assault on beaches within Hagushi Bay. Partially protected bays to the north and south of the Katchin Peninsula on Okinawa's eastern side were Chimu and Nakagusuku Bays (the latter subsequently re-named 'Buckner Bay'). These east-coast bays were identified as potential naval bases and staging areas for the Home Islands' invasion as they were the only substantial fleet anchorages between Kyushu and Formosa.

Okinawa is oriented north-east to south-west. The Motobu Peninsula extends into the East China Sea at the island's widest (18 miles) point. More than half of Okinawa's mass is to the north of the island's narrowest (2 miles) point, the Ishikawa Isthmus, situated near Chimu Wan. Naha, the prefectural capital and commercial centre is located on the western coast and Yonabarua on the east coast to the north of the Chinen Peninsula. Shuri, the Ryukyus ancient, ritual capital is located between the two coasts. The Oroku Peninsula is situated across the Naha Channel from the island's capital. The Kiyamu Peninsula is located at Okinawa's southern tip. (*Meridian Mapping*)

The coast of Okinawa possesses rocky shores in the north, coral reefs in the lowland belt south of the Ishikawa Isthmus, and elevated beaches and seaside cliffs in the south. Thus, the beaches centred on Hagushi, on the western coast between Nagahama and Chatan, were deemed suitable for amphibious assault as well as for their proximity to Yontan and Kadena airfields, a mile inland. Early seizure was to enable land-based American fighters to aid in defending the fleet and to provide close air support for the infantry.

Okinawa did not have a road net, although heavily populated Naha did have some highways. Cross-country vehicular movement was limited to a few single-tracked roads. Tropical heat produced dust while the rainy season (July–November) turned trails to quagmires.

Although the southern part of Okinawa possesses some thinly wooded areas of conifers, the vast bulk of this terrain was cultivated with sugar-cane fields, rice paddies, and farmlands for soybean and sweet potato growth in both the valley and on the hills and plateaus. Okinawa's terrain and vegetation differed from the palm trees, swamps and tropical river deltas that characterised the SPA and SWPA combat since mid-1942.

(**Opposite, above**) Marines wade ashore unopposed over coral reef from an LCVP onto one of the Hagushi beaches on L-Day (Landing Day), 1 April. Much of the Okinawa coastline had scattered coral reefs and low cliffs. The Hagushi beaches were the most desirable landing sites due to their proximity to the Yontan and Kadena airfields and being a few miles south of the island's narrowest point, the Ishikawa Isthmus. (*USMC*)

(**Opposite, below**) An aerial view of Yontan Airfield about a mile inland beyond some elevated ground of 50 feet from the IIIAC landing beaches at Hagushi, to the north of the Bishi Gawa waterway, on the central plains. Another airfield, Kadena, was to the immediate south-east of Yontan and inland from the US 7th Division's beach sector. Machinato Airfield was situated to the north of the prefectural capital city of Naha on Okinawa's western coast. On the eastern coast was the abandoned Yonabaru Airfield. The IJN had an airfield on the Oroku Peninsula, while the US 77th Division captured the two airfields on Ie Shima, to the west of the Motobu Peninsula, on 16–21 April. (*NARA*)

(**Opposite, above**) The 'Awacha Pocket', a gorge that ran through Okinawan ridges in the vicinity of Awacha and Dakeshi. It was situated in the 1st Marine Division's sector north of the IJA 32nd Army's bastion at Shuri in early May. The topography's elevated terrain enabled the Japanese to provide mutually supporting, enfilading gunfire from the 'honeycombs' of caves and dugouts on both sides of the gorge. The 5th Marines, 1st Division fought from 3–11 May to seize this pocket from the remnants of the IJA 62nd Division. (*NARA*)

(**Opposite, below**) Sugar Loaf Ridge was a devastated combat locale that pitted the 6th Marine Division against elements of the IJA 32nd Army. This ridge was east of the prefectural capital of Naha and west of Shuri, the Ryukyu Islands 'ancient', traditional capital and the IJA 32nd Army's headquarters and bastion. Horseshoe and Half Moon Ridges, with Sugar Loaf, comprised the triangle of Japanese fortified elevated positions that plagued the 6th Marine Division. Elsewhere, other steep hills with escarpments and undulating limestone ridges provided excellent mutually supporting elevated defensive lines that suited the enemy's short-range weapons of machine-guns, mortars, 47mm AT guns and other smaller-calibre ordnance. As elsewhere, Sugar Loaf Ridge was 'honeycombed' with crevices and caves cut by underground streams that served as excellent natural fortifications. With extensive hillside tunnelling, the Japanese created a warren of gun positions, personnel quarters and munitions' storage areas. (*NARA*)

(**Above**) A squad of 6th Division Marines atop an Okinawan ridge among scrubby pine trees. They awaited the completion of a preparatory artillery bombardment before making further advances amid the mountainous terrain of the Motobu Peninsula in April. The peninsula had two mountain tracts separated by a central valley that ran east-to-west with the elevated terrain of the Yae-Take ridge complex serving as a natural redoubt for the Japanese defenders, which the Marines overcame on 20 April. (*NARA*)

(**Above**) 77th Division soldiers use a spliced ladder to bridge a gulf between hills during their advance to Shuri in late May. Shuri, with Naha, Itoman and Yonabaru on Okinawa's southern third housed 75 per cent of the island's population. The IJA 32nd Army commanders turned Shuri and its castle into a bastion against the 1st Marine and Army's 77th Divisions' advances. Shuri's heights were an integral part of a defensive corridor that spanned from Naha in the west to Yonabaru on Okinawa's Pacific Ocean coast. From Shuri's high ground, the Japanese had excellent observation over the two coastal regions to provide accurate enfilading fire against the IIIAC Marine Divisions assaults on Sugar Loaf-Horseshoe-Half Moon Ridge complex to the west. (*NARA*)

(**Opposite, above**) An Okinawan village with one of the island's innumerable ridges (*background*). Rural village houses were thatch-roofed and surrounded by stone or mud walls. Village trees and brush blunted the force of winds. However, they also camouflaged Japanese positions. Grain fields and other vegetation near the villages were also transformed into concealed enemy defensive sites to delay the American advance. (*NARA*)

(**Opposite, below**) Narrow Okinawan village streets with crooked offsets to ward off 'evil spirits'. Often entire villages had to be destroyed to facilitate US Tenth Army movement. However, suicidal Japanese defenders concealed in the buildings' ruins still managed to delay the American attack. (*NARA*)

(**Opposite, above**) As some US Tenth Army soldiers move through a recently captured Okinawan village, the remainder of the squad continue to use a wall offset for protection from snipers. An infantryman (*foreground*) carries a Set Complete Radio or Signal Corps Radio (SCR)-536, with a mile's range and dubbed a 'walkie-talkie', which assisted platoon and company level communication for reinforcement and wounded evacuation requests as well as giving map co-ordinates for front-line battalion-level fire missions with mortars and 75mm pack Howitzers. (*NARA*)

(**Opposite, below**) Two Marines train their rifles on the steeple of a destroyed Christian church below Shuri Castle. Every aspect of the natural and man-made terrain features was used by the Japanese to delay the advance of the US 1st Marine and 77th Divisions onto Shuri, which was transformed into a major, centrally placed anchor of the IJA 32nd Army's defensive line spanning the island's width. (*NARA*)

(**Above**) Marines follow an M4 tank past a telephone pole (*background*) along a paved road in Naha. Okinawan locales were interconnected to larger population centres by a network of single-track roads and trails. A two-lane limestone road was constructed between Naha and Shuri before the war. (*NARA*)

(**Opposite, above**) Squad members of 6th Marine Division's Company G, 2nd Battalion, 22nd Marines take cover behind the walls of a ruined building in Naha with a nearby 0.30-inch calibre Browning LMG position behind some of the city's debris. Naha underwent extensive preparatory aerial, ground and naval bombardment. The 6th Marines Division's attack on Naha was in stark tactical contrast to the recent gruelling combat at Sugar Loaf-Horseshoe-Half Moon Ridge complex before the axis of advance was shifted west towards the urban centre. (*NARA*)

(**Opposite, below**) A 22nd Marines Mine Disposal Engineers unit uses an SCR-625 metal detector to locate Japanese mines along a Naha road before an M4 medium tank (*background*) moves forward. The SCR-625 mine detector, weighing 8lb, consisted of a 6-foot pole attached to an 18-inch-diameter wooden disc with a cylindrical search coil underneath capable of detecting metal mines up to a foot below ground. The metal mine detector was ineffective against wooden or plastic mines, which made the engineers' job difficult and time-consuming as bayonet-probing became necessary. (*NARA*)

(**Above**) Two 22nd Marines Mine Disposal Engineers hoist a Japanese Model 96 (1936) landmine after its excavation. The mine was over 10 inches in height with a 20-inch diameter. Its total weight could exceed 100lb with 45lb of explosive charge. Two lead alloy horns (removed with de-fusing) enclosed glass vials containing an electrolyte solution, which when crushed by the pressure of a tank activated a chemical-electric detonator. (*NARA*)

A supply line of 22nd Marines, 6th Marine Division manhandles artillery shells up a muddy incline during their advance onto Naha amid the torrential rains of late May. Prior to Naha's assault, the 6th Marine Division's three regiments (22nd, 29th and 4th Marines) combated tenacious, interlocking Japanese defensive positions along a triangularly situated ridge-line comprising elevated terrain features called 'Sugar Loaf', 'Horseshoe' and 'Half Moon' Ridges. (*NARA*)

(**Opposite, above**) Two Marines view the destroyed treads of a mud-encased M4 medium tank disabled by a Japanese landmine, which served as a stark reminder of the Japanese infantryman's suicidal ferocity against American IIIAC and XXIV Corps armour. At Kazazu Ridge in mid-April, in the US 27th Division sector, over thirty US M4 and M7 medium tanks and HMC of the 193rd and 713th Tank Battalions ran into landmines and a tenacious IJA 272nd Independent Battalion attack with TNT satchels, grenades and small-arms. In all, twenty-two tanks were destroyed and the 193rd Tank Battalion never returned to combat. (*NARA*)

(**Opposite, below**) 77th Division infantrymen march along a rain-soaked muddy road past some stalled M8 HMCs during US Tenth Army's advance southward towards the IJA 32nd Army's Japanese Shuri defences during the latter half of May. On Shuri's eastern side, the 77th Division contested Japanese positions along ridge-lines named 'Chocolate Drop' and 'Flat Top' in the vicinity of Ishimmi. (*NARA*)

(**Above**) An American infantryman slides down a rain-soaked muddy hill during the latter part of the Tenth Army's southern offensive on Shuri in May. An officer of the 96th Infantry Division quipped about his troops' movement over the terrain's morass amid flooded roads: 'Those on the forward slopes slid down. Those on the reverse slopes slid back.' *(NARA)*

(**Opposite, above**) To the west of Shuri, riflemen from the 1st Battalion, 29th Marines, 6th Division follow an M4 medium flame-throwing tank between the embankments of a destroyed railway track. Thirty miles of a narrow-gauge railroad connected Naha to Shuri and other locales such as Yonabaru, Itoman, Kokuba and Kadena. Branches of the line were re-constructed by American engineers. *(NARA)*

(**Opposite, below**) Two Marines of Company C, 22nd Marines, 6th Division scan the outskirts of Naha from a foxhole on the northern bank of the Asato River. During the morning hours of 14 May, the 22nd and elements of the 29th Marines seized over 1,000 yards of the river's bank, despite the presence of numerous Japanese machine-gun and sniper pits. *(NARA)*

Riflemen from the 22nd Marines, 6th Division cross the Asa River's partially destroyed bridge on the way to Naha, under enemy sniper fire. During the night of 10–11 May, the 6th Marine Division engineers erected a Bailey bridge across the river, enabling tanks and heavy weapons to support the Marine assault. The 22nd Marines and supporting armour were under constant artillery fire from well-sited Japanese positions on Shuri Heights' western face. Another Bailey bridge was constructed days later across the Asato River to replace a demolished stone bridge to support Marine armour movement onto Naha. (NARA)

27th Division soldiers cross a footbridge on the Machinato Inlet, a low flat area covered with rice paddies and dissected by streams, during the early morning of 19 April after a massive XXIV Corps artillery preparatory bombardment. The inlet's crossing, to the north-east of the Machinato Airfield along Okinawa's western coast, was the opening movement along the entire XXIV Corps front. There the 27th, 77th and 96th Divisions were to contest the IJA 32nd Army on several entrenched hill masses including Kazazu, Nishibaru, Tanabaru Ridges as well as the Maeda Escarpment to the north of the Naha-Shuri-Yonabaru defence-line. (NARA)

Three Marines inspect a Japanese soldier's *Arisaka* rifle found in a dry water basin used to collect rainwater for nearby rice paddies' irrigation. Unfortunately, these concrete-lined basins served as concealed man-made enemy fortifications. (NARA)

67

(**Opposite, above**) A squad of Marines without field packs carefully advance along the lip of a rice paddy towards enemy positions near a wooded area (*background*). Some areas of Okinawa were lightly wooded, but the majority of the island's flat valley terrain, mostly in the south, was cultivated with a variety of crops, especially rice. (*NARA*)

(**Opposite, below**) A squad of Marines advance towards a wooded area beyond a grain field. The Okinawans grew grain, sweet potato, sugar-cane and soybeans in the valley fields, which often had wooded areas left intact as windbreaks. For the advancing Americans, crops approaching near-complete height served as natural terrain areas for enemy concealment. (*NARA*)

(**Above**) Several Marines gather around a wounded Japanese soldier captured in a sugar-cane field, in mid-June. The height of the crop was extensive at spring's end, enabling enemy soldiers and even small ordnance such as mortars and 47mm AT guns to be concealed there. (*NARA*)

(**Opposite, above**) An American M4 medium tank and accompanying infantry move up a draw with an enemy controlled hill mass in the background. In southern Okinawa, irregular hills and knolls (*background*) dotted the terrain, could be as high as 500 feet and were tenaciously defended by the enemy. Caves created by underground streams appeared as 'honeycombs' on the hills' faces. The draw's flat terrain provided an excellent field of fire from the enemy-held hill mass with their concealed shorter-range weapons, such as mortars, AT and machine-guns, all of which had devastating effects on advancing US armour and infantry in the open. (*NARA*)

(**Opposite, below**) In an iconic image, a 29-year-old father of four, Marine Pfc. Paul E. 'Pop' Ison of L Company, the 3rd Battalion, 5th Marines, 1st Division runs across an open, 75-yard area called 'Death Valley', on 10 May. He was part of a four-man team sent to destroy an enemy pillbox. On this day, during an eight-hour period, the Marines suffered 125 casualties crossing this particular valley in rough terrain, which became known as the 'Awacha Pocket', north-east of Dakeshi and south of the town of Awacha. (*USMC*)

(**Above**) Marines take cover from Japanese sniper fire behind Okinawan burial structures along Cemetery Ridge in early June. These ceremonial monuments were often the only sites in the open for American infantry to use as cover against enemy small-arms gunfire. (*USMC*)

The field of fire overlooking a sugar-cane field as viewed from the interior of an Okinawan burial tomb after its capture. These fortified tombs had to be reduced one at a time by the advancing Tenth Army formations. (NARA)

(**Opposite, above**) Advancing XXIV Corps infantry take cover behind an Okinawan ritual animal statue along the top of a hill's forward face during the last few days of the campaign, in mid-June. (USAMHI)

(**Opposite, below**) Two Marines carefully examine an Okinawan burial tomb. Many of these ritualistic sites were fortified as Japanese strongpoints requiring either direct gunfire from tanks or 37mm AT guns as well as explosive satchels to overcome them. (NARA)

(**Opposite, above**) A well-camouflaged opening to a Japanese LMG position. Such emplacements covered the Marines' southward approach against the tenaciously held ridgeline between Naha and Shuri, in May. Advancing American infantry would be unable to detect the position until almost atop it. (*NARA*)

(**Opposite, below**) A bunkered position carved into the limestone of a ridge and reinforced with a log embrasure. The slit-like opening was able to house a HMG and withstand small-arms fire. Direct tank or 37mm AT gunfire as well as flame-throwers and explosive satchels were needed to reduce these stone-fortified positions. (*NARA*)

(**Above**) Marines from the 6th Division on the Motobu Peninsula inspect a Japanese 5-inch naval gun encased in a concrete and limestone emplacement dug into the base of a hill during combat there in mid-April. The narrowness of the embrasure made it difficult to detect with aerial reconnaissance and the stone fortification necessitated direct gunfire with multiple strikes to reduce it. (*NARA*)

(**Opposite, above**) A Marine stands in the foreground of the reverse slope of Machisi Hill near Naha. Elements of the 4th Marines, 6th Division assaulted this hill after receiving long-range machine-gun and rifle fire from this height on 23–24 May. This ridge was about 500 yards south of the Asato River in the vicinity of Machisi. The many Okinawan tombs on the reverse slope were fortified with mortar emplacements, while the face of the height was studded with machine-guns. (*NARA*)

(**Opposite, below**) A pair of Marines from the 2nd Battalion of the 6th Marine Division's Reconnaissance Company prepare to assault a Japanese-occupied cave on the Oroku Peninsula south of Naha in early June. The Marine on the right was about to hurl a hand-grenade through the cave's opening while a rifleman on the left waited with his M1 Garand semi-automatic weapon for any fleeing enemy. (*NARA*)

(**Above**) A Japanese 150mm Model 89 (1929) field gun in its concrete and wood emplacement dug into a hill's cave on the Motobu Peninsula. Wooden planking was situated beneath the cannon's wheels to facilitate its movement to the cave's opening for firing. (*NARA*)

(**Above**) Japanese concrete-walled and steel/timber-reinforced ceilings were the main fortified elements to this shelter for enemy light AA guns and personnel in the vicinity of the Naha Airfield on the Oroku Peninsula. This fortified shelter was found by Marines on 15 June. Large, heavily reinforced tunnels scattered throughout Okinawa served as command bunkers, hospitals, ammunition dumps and troop quarters. Admiral Ota's headquarters was a virtual underground warren that contained more than 1,500 feet of tunnels connected to galleries, galleys and other rooms. These underground areas were also equipped with ventilation and electricity. Interconnected, complex cave positions, such as these were destroyed when Tenth Army engineers, over a few days, pumped up to 700 gallons of gasoline into the entrance and set off the fire and explosion with a tracer round or a phosphorus grenade. In this manner, the blast and ensuing inferno killed the enemy defenders while the cave was sealed from within. (*NARA*)

(**Opposite, above**) Deception methods as well as structural fortifications were part of the Japanese preparations for the American invasion. Above, two wooden dummy Japanese fighters are shown as they were parked under camouflage netting at Yontan Airfield to confuse the Allies of the enemy air strength. (*NARA*)

(**Opposite, below**) A XXIV Corps soldier examines a wooden dummy Japanese tank that was discovered under some unscathed trees as part of deception methods to confuse the Americans about the strength and location of enemy armour. (*NARA*)

A dead barefooted Japanese soldier lays sprawled in a field after being killed by sentries while infiltrating American lines. His *Arisaka* rifle and unattached bayonet are next to the corpse. Colonel Nariake Arisaka developed a new bolt action rifle in 1907 that remained in continuous production to 1944. The original 6.5mm cartridge did not have the same range or stopping power as the larger Allied rifle, so a 7.7mm round was developed. (*NARA*)

A Marine removes HE stick-hand-grenades from the corpse of a female IJA nurse at Kunishi Ridge near the island's west coast in the Marines' IIIAC sector. The handle of this grenade was much shorter than German models and was ignited by pulling a cord at the base of the stick. The nurse carried ammunition and bandages in another pouch. (*NARA*)

A Japanese soldier was captured wearing civilian clothes as he tried to infiltrate US 27th Division lines to detonate explosives. With organised resistance by the IJA 32nd Army waning in the Kiyamu Peninsula in the latter part of June, General Ushijima exhorted some of his officers and enlisted men to don Okinawan garb in an attempt to reach the northern part of the island rather than surrender or commit ritualistic suicide. (*Author's Collection*)

Marine flares illuminated the night sky over Okinawa in order to detect enemy positions and areas of infiltration. Both Marine and army mortars were capable of firing illumination rounds. *(NARA)*

A captured Japanese explosive satchel charge that could serve as a crude landmine or AT weapon. For the latter, suicidal Japanese infantrymen, often under the cover of smoke, charged American tanks and hurled the 20lb charge under the hull or onto the treads. (*NARA*)

A Marine welds additional steel tank treads onto the glacis plate of an M4 medium tank. Also affixed to a hull's sides were 2-inch-thick wood planks for added protection. Japanese infantry suicide squads, after separating American infantry from their tanks, rushed to place Model 99 magnetic explosive charges onto the armoured vehicle's hull. (*NARA*)

(**Above**) A Marine M4 medium tank with additional welded hull and turret steel treads. American tank losses were extremely heavy at such locales as Kakazu Ridge in mid-April during an advance by elements of the US 27th Division. IJA suicide demolition squads destroyed over a score of US 193rd Tank Battalion's M4 medium tanks there. (*NARA*)

(**Opposite, above**) A Marine inspects captured Japanese suicide or Q-boats in their cave revetments at Naha. These speedy (20-knot), small plywood craft were 18 feet long and 5 feet in width and were packed with a 500lb explosive charge or other lighter depth charges. These vessels were piloted by teenage naval cadets and were unleashed to wreak havoc on the Allied armada. Only a few small American ships were damaged or sunk. (*NARA*)

(**Opposite, below**) One-man piloted rocket-propelled aircraft were found near Kadena Airfield on 3 April. This IJN *Yokosuka* MXY-7 craft was to be dropped at 20,000 feet by a G4M (Betty) bomber and then dive onto Allied shipping as a three-rocket-propelled 'flying bomb' at over 600mph. This suicide aircraft's nose warhead carried up to 4,000lb of HE. Only a few inflicted damage on the offshore armada as most of the G4M (Betty) bombers were shot down with the MXY-7s affixed. (*USAMHI*)

"BAKA" bomb?

(**Above**) An IJN Mitsubishi A6M Reisen fighter (Zero or Zeke) on a *kamikaze* mission with some of its tail destroyed in the vicinity of the USS *Essex* on 14 May. Another IJN carrier-borne dive-bomber, the Yokosuka D4Y Suisei (Judy), and the Nakajima Ki-115 (Tsurugi or Toka) were *kamikaze* aircraft. Over 1,900 suicidal sorties were unleashed with a 15 per cent success rate at hitting an Allied ship. US picket destroyers suffered grievously, while some Allied carriers were set ablaze. (*NARA*)

(**Opposite, above**) A damaged Japanese bomber and the corpse of an enemy commando (*foreground*) at Yontan Airfield. A seventy-member suicide airborne commando force, carried by five twin-engined (Sally) bombers flew to Yontan late on 24 May. All but one that 'belly-landed' (above) were shot down. The surviving Sally's commandos exited and hurled demolitions and grenades at the closest American planes, destroying or damaging thirty-three aircraft. Over 70,000 gallons of aviation fuel was set ablaze. Chaotic defensive ground-fire killed ten commandos with three others found dead in the bomber. This was the sole enemy airborne attack during the campaign. (*NARA*)

(**Opposite, below**) The IJN battleship *Yamato* (*background*) with nine 18-inch guns is shown with an accompanying destroyer in the East China Sea during 7 April's Operation *Ten-Ichi-Go* (Operation *Heaven One*), a suicidal sortie to bombard the American landing beaches. The IJN light cruiser *Yahagi* also accompanied the battleship. At noon, US carrier aircraft began their attack. (*NARA*)

(**Above**) Smoke billowed from the stricken and capsized *Yamato* on 7 April. American Hellcat, Corsair and Avenger carrier aircraft devastated the battleship with at least eight torpedoes and a dozen bombs during a two-hour aerial assault. The mushroom-shaped smoke-cloud emanated from a massive explosion of the main magazines at 1423hrs. Almost 2,500 IJN sailors perished with their ship, although three surviving IJN destroyers from an escort of eight managed to rescue over 200 seamen from the *Yamato* as well as over 1,300 survivors from the *Yahagi* and the accompanying destroyers sunk. *(NARA)*

(**Opposite**) A Marine on the Oroku Peninsula in early June inspects a Japanese 8-inch-rocket launching site of two narrow-gauge horizontal 15-foot rails situated on a hill's reverse slope. These crude weapons made their debut on Iwo Jima. The aiming and trajectory of these rockets was uncontrolled and by guesswork, which limited accuracy. *(NARA)*

(**Opposite, above**) A Marine patrol on the Oroku Peninsula examines an enemy 8-inch rocket ('Screaming Mimi' or 'Whistling Willie'), which was launched from pairs of narrow-gauge rails often elevated with sandbags. Their characteristic noise was from the friction of the rocket launching over the rails and the end-over-end tumbling flight. The rocket exploded with great concussive force but limited fragmentation. (*NARA*)

(**Opposite, below**) A US 96th Division soldier examines a disabled Japanese light tank in early May after the failed Japanese counter-offensive. Ushijima committed all reserved armour of the IJA 27th Tank Regiment, consisting of limited numbers of Type 95 *Ke-Go* (or *Ha-Go*) 37mm light and Type 97 *Chi-Ha* 57mm medium tanks, on 4 May. The enemy attacked north-westwardly from Yonabaru supporting the counter-offensive in the Maeda-Ishimmi area near the XXIV Corps' 77th and 96th Divisions' boundary. All under-armoured Japanese tanks were easily destroyed by American artillery. (*Author's Collection*)

(**Above**) A Marine brandishes his revolver while examining a dead Japanese soldier at the rear entrance to a ridge's cave. The American war machine needed .38 calibre revolvers for a variety of military and civil roles. Approximately 70,000 Smith & Wesson Model 10 M&P .38 Special revolvers were procured by the US Navy as a 'Victory Model', seeing overseas service among navy pilots and air-crews. Approximately 49,000 Colt .38 calibre Commandos were also purchased during the war for both combat action and among shore personnel. (*NARA*)

(**Above**) A Marine takes cover behind a stone wall from a Japanese sniper in Naha in early June as he held onto the butt-end of his M1 Carbine semi-automatic 0.30- inch calibre rifle. This weapon was originally produced in late 1941 for non-front-line troops, but as it was more effective (15- or 30-round detachable magazine) than a pistol, and lighter (5.2lb unloaded) and more compact rifle than the M1 Garand, its combat use was favoured at close quarters like urban streets or jungle. The carbine fired 45 rounds per minute with an operational range of 275 yards. (*NARA*)

(**Opposite, above**) Two Marines from the 56th Replacement Company, 22nd Marines, 6th Division enter a tomb used for ammunition storage. One cautiously enters the tomb (*right*) while the other (*left*) has his M1 Garand semi-automatic rifle at the ready. The gas-operated M1 Garand entered service in 1936 to replace the Springfield Model 1903 bolt-action rifle. However, it was not widely distributed to soldiers until 1940. After the Guadalcanal campaign, Marine riflemen also adopted the M1 Garand. A firing rate of 40–50 rounds per minute from a stable gun platform with relatively low recoil along with an effective range of over 450 yards were excellent features. However, it weighed 9.6lb (unloaded), a disadvantage, especially for jungle combat. (*NARA*)

(**Opposite, below**) Marine squad members receive stripper clips of 8 rounds of 30.06-inch calibre ammunition for their M1 Garand rifles and hand-grenades. After a rifleman expended the eight rounds, the clip ejected from the gun's internal magazine making a distinctive ping. The standard Mk II 'pineapple' fragmentation hand-grenade was 3.5 inches long and weighed 1.3lb (with 2oz of explosive). The serrated 'pineapple' configuration maximised the grip for the grenade-hurler. The Mark III concussion grenade was cylindrical and contained 8oz of explosive to produce overpressure in confined spaces (bunkers and caves) to stun enemy occupants. (*NARA*)

(**Opposite, above**) An M18 'Hellcat' TD from the AT Company, 306th Infantry Regiment, 77th Division fires its 76mm M1A1 turret gun at an enemy Shuri Line strongpoint in mid-May. The crewman (*right*) was the spotter and machine-gunner for the turret's 0.50-inch calibre HB-M2 HMG and the 0.30-inch calibre M1919A4 LMG. With all Japanese armour destroyed, the M18 was utilised as an assault gun. (*USAMHI*)

(**Opposite, below**) An amphibious LVT (A) moves inland against negligible opposition on L-Day. To counter previously employed (Tarawa, Peleliu) Japanese beach strongpoints, the LVT (A) with its turret M3 75mm Howitzer and two 0.5-inch calibre Browning HMGs was developed. Its maximal speed was 20 and 7.5mph on land and in water, respectively. (*NARA*)

(**Above**) At Wana Ridge in mid-May, a 1st Marines' BAR gunner fires across the terrain's 'moonscape'. The BAR was a squad-level light automatic weapon for suppressive fire using a 0.30-inch calibre cartridge. Its 20-round trapezoidal-shaped magazine was not able to deliver a sustained fire rate. A Marine (*left*) pulls the pin on a hand-grenade to hurl at an enemy position. (*NARA*)

(**Opposite, above**) A machine-gunner from the 2nd Battalion, 1st Marines provides cover-fire with his 0.45-inch calibre Thompson SMG on Wana Ridge's intense combat on 18 May. A division historian noted, 'gains were measured by yards won, lost, then won again'. (*NARA*)

(**Above**) A Marine from the 22nd Marines, 6th Division aims a captured IJN 7.7mm Model 92 machine-gun at the enemy, which was patterned from the venerable Lewis gun of the First World War. Additional ammunition drums and cartons are scattered on the ground nearby. US Coastal Artillery's Colonel Lewis designed this weapon in 1912. By 1915, every British infantry battalion had up to thirty-six Lewis guns. (*NARA*)

(**Opposite, below**) XXIV Corps soldiers leading their dogs: a German shepherd (*left*), a pit bull (*centre*), and a Doberman pinscher (*right*), in search of hiding Japanese soldiers after the failed early May IJA 32nd Army counter-offensive. These dogs, used throughout the Pacific by the Marines too, succeeded in their assigned task of sniffing out lurking enemy soldiers in concealed positions. (*NARA*)

(**Opposite, above**) Marines from Company A, 2nd Battalion, 5th Marines, 1st Division use an M1 2.36-inch rocket-launcher ('bazooka') against fortified Japanese positions in the 'Awacha 'Pocket's' irregular terrain in early May. Note the other Marines taking cover on both sides of the bazooka's firer to avoid the 'backblast' after the projectile was discharged. (*NARA*)

(**Opposite, below**) A pair of soldiers prepare to fire one of their new weapons, the M18 57mm man-portable recoilless rifle (RCL), to be used against Japanese pillboxes on Okinawa. This weapon fired a high explosive (HE) 5.3lb projectile, an HE Anti-Tank (HEAT) one, or smoke. The M18 worked on the same principle as the bazooka, but was slightly larger, more powerful with a greater effective range. It could be fired from a monopod, bipod or from the shoulder. The Browning M1917A1 machine-gun's tripod also served as a useful mount for the M18 RCL. (*USAMHI*)

(**Above**) The US Tenth Army commander, General Simon B. Buckner, utilised a term, 'blowtorch and corkscrew' to describe the campaign's main infantry tactic shown above. Liquid flame ('blowtorch') and explosives ('corkscrew') were employed by small units to destroy Japanese strongholds' defenders. After throwing an explosive charge into an enemy position on the Oroku Peninsula, a 6th Division Marine sent in a jet of flame from his weapon while another stood at the ready with his rifle for any escaping Japanese. (*NARA*)

(**Opposite, above**) A Marine M4 medium sends a high-pressured jet of flame from its 75mm gun barrel. The flame-throwing tank, supported by Marine riflemen, was combating enemy caves on the face of a ridge. The tank contained 300 gallons of flammable napalm and gasoline, which the gun delivered between 80–125 yards. The greater composition of napalm made the mixture more viscous. *(NARA)*

(**Opposite, below**) Marines take cover after detonating a large explosive device. The normal tactic in cave and pillbox assault incorporated infantry-demolition teams supported by direct fire weapons such as tanks, flame-throwers and 37mm AT guns. Cave positions were frequently neutralised by sealing the entrances with an explosive detonation. *(NARA)*

(**Above**) Two Marine snipers behind an earthen breastwork apply their craft at 600 yards utilising the USMC M1903A4 Springfield sniper rifle with a Unertl scope. The M1903 Springfield was favoured over the Winchester M70 target rifle and with the scope's optics enhanced by employing an 8 × target scope (made by John Unertl) rather than a lower magnification hunting telescope, it became the 'sniping standard' for the USMC in the Pacific. *(NARA)*

(**Above**) A Marine gunner holds a pistol grip and fires his Browning M1919A4 0.30-inch calibre LMG at enemy positions atop another ridge in early May. This platoon or company-level machine-gun was situated on a tripod, was air-cooled with a perforated jacket surrounding the barrel, and fed by a 150-round ammunition fabric belt that was inserted by opening the top cover. (*NARA*)

(**Opposite, above**) A twin 0.30-inch calibre air-cooled machine-gun-crew with the guns mounted on a tripod and 250-round belt-fed ammunition at the ready. The M1919 LMG gun had an effective range of 1,500 yards with a rate of fire of 400–600 rounds per minute. (*NARA*)

(**Opposite, below**) A Browning M1917A water-cooled MMG with its three-Marine crew. This venerable weapon was deployed in the First World War as the Browning M1917 and weighted just over 100lb including the gun, tripod, water for cooling the barrel and a standard supply of 0.30-inch calibre ammunition in metal containers. The M1917A refined Browning's successful design with an improved bottom plate and an increased firing rate of 600 rounds per minute. Its effective range was over 1,500 yards, making it an excellent fixed-position defensive weapon and one for suppressive fire. (*NARA*)

(**Above**) Three Marines of L Company, 22nd Marines, 6th Division bring up ammunition belts and containers of 0.30-inch calibre ammunition for their machine-gun positions in May during the assault on the Sugar Loaf-Half Moon-Horseshoe Ridge complex. (*NARA*)

(**Opposite, below**) Marine 1-ton trucks fire their 4.5-inch rockets on the Naha-Shuri Line in May. These trucks mounted three M7 rocket launcher racks, each of which held twelve HE rockets with a range of 1,100 yards. A Marine division was furnished with twelve of these vehicles. (*NARA*)

A tracked light infantry vehicle made by Studebaker, the M29 'Weasel' crosses over a Bailey bridge days after the unopposed invasion. The 'Weasel' was introduced for the First Special Services Force *"DEVIL'S BRIGADE"* who were training to move quickly (top speed 36mph) across Norway's snowy terrain to attack Nazi 'heavy water' plants. Although never used in Norway, it was adapted to carry arms, explosives and supplies as well as serve as an ambulance over muddy terrain. Due to its lighter weight, it was also able to cross minefields and not detonate Japanese AT mines. *(NARA)*

(**Opposite, above**) A Marine 37mm AT gun fires at entrenched Japanese positions. Often when Marine armour was not able to advance to reduce Japanese fortified cave positions by point-blank gunfire, these near-obsolete weapons by ETO standards proved their utility with a short-range, HE shell, which was also effective against thinly armoured enemy tanks. Against massed Japanese infantry assaults, the 37mm gun, when loaded with canister, acted like a 'giant shotgun' that decimated the enemy's ranks. (*NARA*)

(**Above**) A 15th Marines' M8 75mm pack Howitzer of the 6th Marine Division during a counter-battery duel on the Oroku Peninsula near Toma in early June when Marine armour was unable to move forward to silence enemy guns. The 15th Marines, firing against Japanese gun flashes, silenced four 120mm dual-purpose, one 6-inch, and several smaller calibre enemy field guns. The utility of this weapon was that it could be stripped down into component parts in seconds for animal packs (thus, the term 'pack Howitzer') or human transport. The M8, with its metal wheels and rubber tyres, was introduced in 1936 for mountain and paratroop formations. This relatively light 1,300lb Howitzer, which fired HE ammunition in support of infantry, was also useful at disrupting advancing enemy formations and concentration areas. (*NARA*)

(**Opposite, below**) A Marine 105mm Howitzer fires a round into Naha on 27 May. A destroyed building on the city's outskirts is in the background. Colonel Shapeley's 4th Marines, just before their relief by the 29th Marines the next day, were to move onto the rest of Naha, following a nine-battalion preparatory artillery bombardment of suspected Japanese positions in Naha. (*NARA*)

(**Opposite, above**) A Marine M1 155mm Howitzer crew after just firing at round at the IJA 32nd Army's final redoubts at the southern end of Okinawa in mid-June. This ordnance was designed for vehicular transport (weight over 12,000lb) and had a split trail and a small protective shield. The 155mm was able to hurl a 95lb HE shell over 15,000 yards. (*NARA*)

(**Above**) Two Marines fire a round out of their 60mm M2 mortar from a shallow, partially concealed weapon-pit adjacent to a grain-field on the front-lines in mid-May. The M2 mortar was a simple system for use at company and platoon levels for immediate close infantry support. It was capable of firing HE, smoke and illumination shells at a rate of over 18 rounds per minute. (*NARA*)

(**Opposite, below**) A Marine 81mm M1 mortar team of the 3rd Battalion, 22nd Marines' Headquarters Company, 6th Division fires an HE round (comparable to a 105mm shell) from a shallow pit behind the reverse slope of a hill. This mortar crew, positioned in relatively open terrain, attested to the need for rapid deployment of these weapons with their 'plunging fire' on enemy positions in support of assaulting Marine riflemen. The 81mm M1 mortar was the most powerful infantry weapon at the battalion level. (*NARA*)

(**Opposite, above**) A Marine examines the shrapnel-laced ruins of an 81mm M1 mortar pit that was completely destroyed by Japanese artillery fire resulting in three American casualties. A Marine's helmet and a pair of boots are situated in the mud near the tube along with destroyed ammunition cans and mortar rounds during combat on the Naha-Shuri Line in the third week of May. (NARA)

(**Above**) A crew from the US 7th Division's 91st Chemical Company (Separate) amid Naha's ruins with their M2 4.2-inch mortar, who supported the 6th Marine Division's Oroku Peninsula's invasion on 7 June. The Marines, which did not have the 4.2-inch mortar in their armamentarium, valued this weapon's placement of HE and white phosphorus rounds on enemy positions. This heavy mortar was designed to hurl a 20lb round and entered service in 1943. Its 4-foot tube, weighing 105lb, was rifled and the weapon had a range of 560 to 4,400 yards. Rounds were fired onto enemy positions along reverse slopes with 'plunging' bombardment rather than direct fire. As it was extremely difficult to transport more cumbersome field artillery pieces over rough terrain, the 4.2-inch mortar was quite versatile. The 4.2-inch mortars were able to be mounted in landing craft to assist as fire support in the amphibious assaults of Okinawa's offshore islands. (NARA)

(**Opposite, below**) The Chance-Vought F4U *Corsair* was one of the great combat aeroplanes of the war. The plane possessed speed and a formidable attack platform with six 0.5-inch calibre machine-guns plus two 1,000lb bombs or eight 5-inch rockets. Its maximal speed approached 420mph at 20,000 feet (maximal ceiling 37,000 feet). In addition to combat ruggedness, it had a range of 1,000 miles. Here, a *Corsair* of MAG 31 fires its rockets at Japanese positions on southern Okinawa. (USMC)

(**Above**) A US Navy TBF Avenger torpedo-bomber drops 500lb bombs on Japanese positions. Despite an inauspicious debut at the Battle of Midway in June 1942, the Avenger became the Navy's classic torpedo bomber of the war. The aircraft had two 0.50-inch calibre forward-firing machine-guns in the leading edges of the wings, a rearward-facing trainable defensive one in the dorsal turret as well as a 0.30-inch calibre machine-gun in the ventral position for its crew of three. The Avenger was able to carry a 2,500lb bomb or torpedo load. (*NARA*)

(**Opposite, above**) A US Navy Grumman F6F Hellcat fighter after crashing at Yontan Airfield following landing-gear failure. This carrier-based aircraft replaced the F4F Wildcat and became the major fighter of the Navy during the second half of the Pacific War after its debut in September 1943. The Hellcat outperformed a captured IJN A6M Reisen ('Zero' or 'Zeke') during test flights. (*NARA*)

(**Opposite, below**) A radioman and two Marine observers direct fire against fortified Japanese positions along the Shuri Line at the end of May from their nearby M7 105mm HMC. Additional tank tracks mounted on the side of the HMC afforded the crew more armoured protection from Japanese 47mm AT guns and other ordnance. The radioman is carrying the standard SCR-300 backpack radio with telephone handset for field communication at the company level. (*NARA*)

(**Opposite, above**) Soldiers of the 77th Division stand in the rain next to a radio mounted on a truck on 8 May. These soldiers, veterans of the Maeda Escarpment (Hacksaw Ridge) battle, were listening to a broadcast of the German surrender in the ETO. (*NARA*)

(**Opposite, below**) A Marine fire control director with his radar direction finder at the Naha Airfield on the Oroku Peninsula after its capture. As picket ships in the US Navy suffered the heaviest attrition and casualties from Japanese *kamikaze* attacks, land-based radar was installed on Okinawa as quickly as possible. (*NARA*)

(**Above**) A variety of radar devices at the emplacements of the 8th AA Artillery Battalion's Battery C along Nago Bay at the southern shoreline of the Motobu Peninsula on 27 June. The Signal Corps Radio (SCR)-584 (*foreground*) was an automatic-tracking microwave ground-based radar unit at the end of the Pacific War. The SCR-584 was initially deployed at Anzio in February 1944 where it played a key role in disrupting the *Luftwaffe's* large air attacks on the Allied beach-head. By the end of the war, these radar devices were used to track artillery shells in flight, detect vehicles, and reduced the manpower needed to guide AA guns. (*USAMHI*)

(**Opposite, above**) A Marine Fighter Squadron of Chance-Vought F4U Corsairs (VMF-311, 'Hell's Bells') of MAG-31, 4th MAW in silhouette outlined by AA tracer rounds fired against a night-time Japanese air-raid at Yontan Airfield on 16 April. As the speedy Corsair was a difficult plane to land on a carrier (compared to the Hellcat), the US Navy relegated this superb fighter to a Marine land-based role at Yontan Airfield. VMF-311, led by Major Michael R. Yunck, landed at Yontan on 7 April. This squadron was credited with destroying seventy-one enemy aircraft with Yunck and Second-Lieutenant William P. Brown, Jr. being awarded Navy Crosses after becoming aces with five and seven kills, respectively. Both pilots flew in Korea where Brown was killed in action and received his second Navy Cross posthumously. (*NARA*)

(**Opposite, below**) Crewmen of the USS *Missouri*, an *Iowa*-class battleship, react in awe from within their 40mm Bofors gun turrets as a Japanese *kamikaze* A6M Reisen ('Zero' or 'Zeke') fighter prepared to crash into the ship on 11 April. Minor damage was suffered to the battleship's starboard side just below her main deck. The *Missouri* had participated in the naval bombardment of Okinawa's south-eastern coast in March and April, destroying many Japanese positions and industrial sites. During the Okinawa campaign, 'Big Mo' shot down several Japanese aircraft and repelled daylight enemy raiding boats. Imperial Japan's surrender was signed in Tokyo Bay on 2 September on the decks of the USS *Missouri*. (*Author's Collection*)

(**Above**) The flight deck of the USS *Bunker Hill*, an Essex-class carrier, ablaze after two *kamikaze* fighters attacked the vessel on 11 May. Casualties exceeded 600 officers and seamen with over 350 confirmed dead. (*NARA*)

The veteran USS *Intrepid*, another of the twenty-four Essex-class carriers built during the war, billows smoke after a *kamikaze* plane's 500lb bomb penetrated the aft flight deck and entered the engine room killing eight men and wounding twenty-one on 16 April. A screening Fletcher-class destroyer (*foreground*) steamed nearby to support the stricken carrier and remove casualties and search for sailors overboard. Within an hour, the flaming gasoline was extinguished and three hours after the *kamikaze* attack, the *Intrepid* began landing its own aircraft. (*NARA*)

Crewmen aboard the USS *Birmingham*, a Cleveland-class light cruiser commissioned in January 1943 that saw extensive action in both the Mediterranean and Pacific theatres, wield a water hose and examine damage to the ship's deck after a *kamikaze* plane's 500lb bomb struck the No. 2 turret on 4 May after the warship had fought off earlier aerial attacks by Japanese suicide pilots that day. Fifty-two crew members were killed with another eighty-two wounded in the attack. Total US Navy casualties aboard ships off Okinawa were 9,731, of whom 4,907 were killed, most of them by *kamikaze* attacks. (*NARA*)

Chapter Three

Commanders and Combatants

The overall strategic commander for Okinawa's invasion was Fleet Admiral Chester W. Nimitz, while Admiral Raymond A. Spruance commanded both the Fifth Fleet and the Central Pacific TF, including TF 50 with its Covering Forces and Special Groups. Vice-Admiral (promoted to Admiral in May 1945) Richmond Kelly Turner commanded the Joint Expeditionary Force (TF 51), totalling more than 1,200 ships. The Fast Carrier Force (TF 58) was commanded by Vice-Admiral Marc A. 'Pete' Mitscher, while the British Carrier Force (TF 57) was commanded by Vice-Admiral Sir H. Bernard Rawlings, RN. Both of these forces were to conduct preparatory airstrikes against Okinawa's defences and neutralise the Japanese air assets before the invasion.

The US Tenth Army was under the command of the Army's Lieutenant-General Simon Bolivar Buckner, Jr, the son of a Confederate general during the American Civil War. Buckner, a West Point graduate, had earlier in the war commanded the forces retaking the Aleutian Islands from the Japanese. As Tenth Army commander, Buckner commanded both Marines and Army units for Operation *Iceberg* designated as 'Expeditionary Troops and Tenth Army, TF 56'.

The immediate naval support for Tenth Army comprised two landing task forces: a Northern Attack Force (TF 53), led by Rear-Admiral Lawrence R. Reifsnider, a veteran naval commander of many Marine amphibious assaults; and a Southern Attack Force (TF 55), under Rear-Admiral John L. Hall, Jr. Reifsnider's TF 53 was to land Major-General Roy S. Geiger's IIIAC consisting of the battle-hardened (Guadalcanal, Cape Gloucester, Peleliu) 1st ('the Old Breed') and newly formed 6th Marine Divisions under the commands of Major-Generals Pedro A. del Valle, a Guadalcanal 11th Marines artillery commander, and future 20th Marine Corps Commandant Lemuel C. Shepherd, respectively. Shepherd, a 5th Marines' veteran in France in 1917, commanded the 9th Marines as part of the newly formed 3rd Marine Division for the Pacific War. Then he served as assistant commander, 1st Marine Division for the Cape Gloucester assault in December 1943. In May 1944, Shepherd led the 1st Provisional Marine Brigade during the Guam invasion in July–August 1944 before organising the 6th Marine Division (from the 1st Provisional Marine Brigade nucleus) for Okinawa.

Geiger, the successful Marine aviation commander from the Guadalcanal campaign, led IMAC for the Bougainville invasion at Empress Augusta Bay under Vice-Admiral William F. Halsey in November 1943. After Bougainville, IMAC was re-designated IIIAC, which Geiger led for the Guam and Peleliu invasions in the Marianas and Palaus, respectively. The 2nd Marine Division served as a demonstration force off Okinawa and then as a floating reserve. The division's 8th Marines Special Landing Force secured offshore islands in June 1945 before being attached to the 1st Marine Division at the end of the Okinawa campaign.

The 1st Marine Division's 1st, 5th and 7th Marines were revered as the 'Old Breed', since it contained almost 6,000 officers and enlisted men who had served during the Pacific campaign for almost three years. The newly formed 6th Marine Division also contained many Pacific veterans, becoming activated in September 1944 around the nucleus of the 1st Provisional Marine Brigade, comprising the 4th and 22nd Marines, who had landed on Guam. The 4th Marines had elements of former Marine Raider battalions, victorious veterans of Guadalcanal, New Georgia and Bougainville. The 22nd Marines had campaigned in the Eniwetok and Guam landings in the Marshall and Mariana Islands, respectively. Elements of the 29th Marines had been attached to the 2nd Marine Division for the Saipan invasion in the Marianas. The 2nd Marine Division was a veteran formation of Guadalcanal, Tarawa, Saipan and Tinian invasions.

Hall's TF 55 was charged with transporting the Army's XXIV Corps, under the command of Major-General John R. Hodge. XXIV Corps comprised the US 7th (commanded by Major-General Archibald V. Arnold) and 96th (led by Major-General James L. Bradley) Divisions, both veteran formations of the Leyte campaign. Hodge had extensive combat experience campaigning alongside Marine units as the assistant commander of the US Army's 25th Division on Guadalcanal. After promotion to major-general in April 1943, he replaced Major-General John H. Hester as the commander of the US 43rd Infantry Division on New Georgia in July 1943. Hodge then led the Americal Division during the bloody Japanese counter-offensive on Bougainville in March 1944. He was next promoted to the XXIV Corps command in April 1944 and participated as part of the US Sixth Army's Leyte campaign. On both Guadalcanal and Bougainville, Hodge and Geiger worked closely together.

The US 7th Division, a regular Army unit, comprised the 17th, 32nd and 184th Infantry Regiments. It had campaigned on Attu in the Aleutians and at Kwajalein in the Marshall Islands. The 96th Division was an army reserve unit that had campaigned on Leyte and comprised the 381st, 382nd and 383rd Infantry Regiments.

Other components to the Okinawa invasion force included: the Western Islands Attack Group (TG 51.1) with the US Army's 77th Division (under Major-General Andrew Bruce); a Demonstration Group (TG 51.2) comprising the 2nd Marine Division (under Major-General Thomas Watson); and the Floating Reserve Groups

(TG 51.3) carrying the US Army's 27th Division (under Major-General George W. Griner, Jr). In order to support the landings along the Hagushi assault beaches, the army's XXIV Corps' 420th Field Artillery Group was to land on Keise Retto to provide long-range artillery support with its 155mm 'Long Tom' cannons.

The 77th Division, an army reserve formation, had fought on both Guam under IIIAC in July 1944 and on Leyte under Sixth Army from December 1944 to February 1945. This formation was to be the first unit to commence Operation *Iceberg* by landing on the Kerama Retto on 26 March 1945. The 27th Division was a New York National Guard unit. It had previously assaulted Saipan under VMAC.

The air component for the initial American assault, Tactical Air Force, Tenth Army, was under the command of Marine Major-General Francis P. Mulcahy, who had led the Cactus Air Force earlier in the Solomon Islands campaign. The 2nd Marine Aircraft Wing (MAW) was to furnish land-based air support once the airfields at Yontan and Kadena were secured.

Okinawa's defence force was the IJA 32nd Army, under the command of Lieutenant-General Mitsuru Ushijima, who although an infantry officer had been a commandant of the Japanese Military Academy as well as a vice minister in the IJA's hierarchy. The IJA 32nd Army was activated on 1 April 1944 and was initially commanded by Lieutenant-General Masao Watanabe. Ushijima, who had earlier combat experience in Burma in 1942 commanding an infantry group, assumed command of the IJA 32nd Army in August 1944.

Prior to April 1944, Okinawa's defence force was mainly a poorly trained garrison. Ushijima committed the main reinforcements from China, Manchuria and Japan for the defences of the Ryukyus, mainly on Okinawa. The IJA 9th Division was a 17,000-man force that had initially been in Manchuria and arrived in June 1944. After American submarine sea-land interdiction had culminated in the sinking of the bulk of the 44th Independent Mixed Brigade's (IMB) transports, resulting in the drowning of 5,000 Japanese soldiers in late June 1944, the IJA 15th IMB was flown in during July. The 44th IMB had to be completely rebuilt as there were only 600 survivors of the naval disaster. The IJA also dispatched the 24th Division (under Lieutenant-General Tatsumi Amamiya) from Manchuria and the 62nd (under the command of Lieutenant-General Takeo Fujioka) from China, the latter in August. However, in mid-January 1945, the IJA 9th Division was transferred from Okinawa to Formosa, which ultimately contributed to the weakened defensive plans for the island.

Major-General (Lieutenant-General in March 1945) Isamu Cho became Ushijima's COS during the summer of 1944 and had come from the Military Affairs Bureau of the War Department in Tokyo. Cho had a fiery aggressive personality, which was in contrast to Ushijima's calm demeanour. Cho had previously commanded a regiment in Manchuria and was linked to the Rape of Nanking incident in 1937. He was also a staff officer in the victorious Malaya and Burma campaigns of 1942. Cho re-organised the IJA 32nd Army's staff, replacing the extant members with younger ones from Tokyo, while retaining Colonel Hiromichi Yahara as the senior staff officer in charge of operations. Yahara had a reputation as a brilliant and decisive tactician. This triumvirate provided the IJA 32nd Army with an impressive leadership balance.

The Japanese strategy was to prolong each inland Okinawan engagement from fixed defences to inflict the greatest number of casualties on the Americans and delay the island's conquest. The previous Japanese military doctrine of always attacking ended in failure on many Pacific battlefields, as did a static defence mode at the surf-side. Okinawa's underground defences and preparations, advocated by Cho, were to prolong the enemy's resistance and were to undermine the Americans' massive advantage in land, sea and air firepower. As such, there was only one armoured unit, the IJA 27th Tank Regiment, consisting of just over a score of *Ha-Go* 37mm light and *Chi-Ha* 57mm medium tanks, but numerous 75mm and 47mm AT guns.

Replete with the 75mm, 100mm and 150mm Howitzer batteries of the IJA 24th Division's 42nd Artillery Regiment, as well as many Japanese units possessing mortars, AA, AT and automatic weapons, the island's 80,000 defenders were prepared to delay almost 500,000 American Marines and soldiers. In addition, there were 5,000 Okinawans conscripts, along with 12,000 Korean labourers.

Rear-Admiral Minoru Ota was in charge of all IJN formations on the island. These included the Okinawa Naval Base Force (under Rear-Admiral Teiso Nippa), the 4th Surface Escort Unit, and various naval aviation formations that in total numbered fewer than 10,000 in strength. Other parts of Ota's command comprised the 27th Torpedo Boat and the 33rd Midget Submarine squadrons as well as a 'suicide boats' or Q-boats unit stationed at Naha. There were also coastal defence companies with 120mm and 140mm guns. In February 1945, Ushijima converted some of Ota's sea-raiding battalions into infantry formations to substitute for the shortage in ground forces after the withdrawal of the IJA 9th Division to Formosa.

(**Opposite, above**) US Navy CPA commanders aboard the USS *Eldorado*, Vice-Admiral Richmond Kelly Turner's (*far right*) flagship. Turner's Joint Expeditionary Force (TF 51) was *Iceberg's* 1,200-ship amphibious arm. Other commanders are (*left-to-right*): Vice-Admiral John H. Hoover, Central Pacific Forward Area; Admiral Raymond A. Spruance, Central Pacific Task Forces and Fifth Fleet; Admiral Chester W. Nimitz, CINCPOA. After Iwo Jima, the *Eldorado* was the Fleet's combat information centre that included Tenth Army commander Lieutenant-General Buckner, until his staff established headquarters on Okinawa after the unopposed Hagushi beaches assault. (*NARA*)

(**Opposite, below**) Admiral William F. Halsey, Commander of the US Navy's Third Fleet (*left*), on Okinawa next to Marine Major-General Francis Mulcahy, commander of the Tenth Army Tactical Air Force. The others comprised Halsey's staff. At the end of providing support for MacArthur's SWPA Luzon campaign, Halsey transferred the Third Fleet to Admiral Spruance on 26 January to be re-designated Fifth Fleet for the Iwo Jima and Okinawa invasions. Command of the Pacific fleet alternated between Halsey and Spruance as American naval and landing forces moved closer in successive campaigns towards Japan. On 27 May, Halsey's Third Fleet resumed responsibility for supporting Tenth Army on Okinawa. The ships and men of the fleet remained the same, only the numerical designations of the TF groups changed. (*NARA*)

Major-General John R. Hodge, US Army XXIV Corps commander (*left*) reviews maps with Tenth Army commander Lieutenant-General Simon B. Buckner, Jr (*right*). Hodge assumed command of the XXIV Corps after Bougainville in April 1944. His XXIV Corps divisions were veterans of the Sixth Army's bloody Leyte campaign that started 20 October 1944. (*NARA*)

Lieutenant-General Simon B. Buckner, Jr, US Tenth Army commander (*far right*), stands at a 6th Marine Division forward OP post on 18 June. Buckner espoused that the infantry's mission was to pin down the enemy and then destroy them with overwhelming firepower. Ironically, soon after this photograph, Buckner was killed by a Japanese artillery shell just days before the island's conquest. (*NARA*)

Lieutenant-General Joseph W. Stilwell (*left*), in his iconic campaign hat, walks to Tenth Army headquarters with interim commander Marine Lieutenant-General Roy S. Geiger. Stilwell replaced the late General Buckner and oversaw the 'mopping-up' of the Japanese resistance on Okinawa during the campaign's waning days. On Okinawa, Stilwell prepared his command for the expected Japanese Home Islands' invasion, making the island functional as a future staging area that included a base for B-29 bombing missions against the enemy homeland. (*NARA*)

Major-General Lemuel C. Shepherd, Jr, 6th Marine Division commander (*centre*), at a forward OP overlooking the Asato River in the drive onto Naha. Immediately behind Shepherd is Lieutenant-Colonel Victor H. Krulak, the division's Assistant COS and G-3 (Operations) with Colonel John C. McQueen (*far left*), the COS. In China before the war, Krulak observed Japanese landing barges with downward-lowering bow ramps (Daihatsu) at the Battle of Shanghai in 1937. With his notes, Krulak later helped design the 'Higgins Boat'. Krulak led the 2nd Marine Parachute Battalion during the Choiseul raid on 28 October–November 4 1943 and was awarded the Navy Cross and Purple Heart with their citations in part stating: 'Assigned the task of diverting hostile attention from the movements of our main attack force *en route* to Empress Augusta Bay, Bougainville Island, Lieutenant-Colonel Krulak … daringly directed the attack of his battalion against the Japanese, destroying hundreds of tons of supplies and burning camps and landing barges. Although wounded … he repeatedly refused to relinquish his command and with dauntless courage and tenacious devotion to duty, continued to lead his battalion against the numerically superior Japanese forces.' When a 6th Marine Division Scout and Sniper reconnaissance company was deployed to western Naha area to relieve the 22nd Marines for action against Japanese positions near Kokuba Hill to the east, Krulak quipped to that unit's commander, Major Anthony 'Cold Steel' Walker (a former Marine Raider): 'Reposing great confidence in your integrity and political ability you are hereby named acting mayor of Naha.' (*NARA*)

Brigadier-General William Clement, the 6th Marine Division's Assistant Commander (*left*) confers with Colonel Merlin F. Schneider, 22nd Marines' commander, outside an HQ tent soon after 5 April's inland move. The 6th Marine Division was tasked with Yontan airfield's capture and to secure Tenth Army's northernmost flank. Schneider's 22nd Marines then pushed inland and seized Okinawa's northern tip at Hedo-Misaki on 13 April. The 22nd Marines eventually moved south to the right of the 1st Marine Division for combat at Sugar Loaf Ridge in late May and after taking heavy casualties, the regiment moved onto Naha. (*NARA*)

(**Above**) Major-General Pedro A. del Valle (*centre*), 1st Marine Division commander, reviews some maps with his staff officers at Sobe on 2 April. An Annapolis graduate, del Valle became the 'first Hispanic Marine general'. After serving as Commander of Marine Forces on Guadalcanal, Tulagi, the Russell and Florida Islands in 1943, del Valle became IIIAC artillery's commander for the Guam invasion. In October 1944, del Valle succeeded Major-General William H. Rupertus, another Guadalcanal veteran, as the 1st Marine Division commander. The 1st Marine Division's 5th and 7th Marines landed at Hagushi along Blue 2 and the Yellow beaches as part of IIIAC's right flank during the amphibious assault on 1 April. The division was then to move quickly eastward towards the Katchin Peninsula to bisect Okinawa with XXIV Corps. (*NARA*)

(**Opposite, above**) Major-General George W. Griner (*right*), the 27th Division's commander is at his HQ. Initially the 27th was part of the Floating Reserve Group (TG 51.3). Its soldiers had participated in the Gilbert and Marshall Islands campaigns prior to landing on Saipan in the Marianas. (*NARA*)

(**Opposite, below**) The Fast Carrier Force (TF 58) was commanded by Vice-Admiral Marc A. 'Pete' Mitscher (*left*) shown aboard the USS *Randolph* on 15 May with his COS, Commodore Arleigh A. Burke. Mitscher's previous flagships, the USS *Enterprise* and *Bunker Hill*, had been damaged by Japanese *kamikaze* planes. Halsey's TF 38 and its fast carriers had bombed Okinawa from October 1944 through January 1945, under the naval air direction of Vice-Admiral John S. McCain. On 27 January, TF 38 reverted to Spruance's command as TF 58 with Mitscher commanding the fast carriers. (*NARA*)

129

Rear-Admiral Clifton A.F. Sprague aboard his flagship USS *Fanshaw Bay*. Sprague previously commanded the USS *Wasp*, before promotion to lead Carrier Division 25 in July 1944. During the Battle of Leyte Gulf, off Samar Island, on 25 October, Sprague's escort carriers ('Taffy 3'), destroyers and destroyer escorts fought off Admiral Takeo Kurita's more powerful IJN force, including the giant battleship *Yamato*. During the melee, Sprague lost four ships sunk and most damaged, but the IJN force turned back. Sprague received the Navy Cross for his offensive-minded leadership. At Okinawa, Sprague commanded Carrier Division 2, with his flag moving to the USS *Ticonderoga* on 1 June. (*NARA*)

A formal posing of IJA and IJN officers on Okinawa with '1' and '2' designating Rear Admiral Minoru Ota, the island's Naval Base Force commander, and Lieutenant-General Mitsuru Ushijima, the IJA 32nd Army leader; '3' identified Major-General Isamu Cho, IJA 32nd Army's COS; '4' and '5' identified Colonel Hitoshi Kanayama, IJA 89th Regiment commander; and Colonel Kiuji Hongo, IJA 32nd Regiment commander. Colonel Hirimichi Yahara, a senior IJA 32nd Army staff operations officer is shown as '6'. (*NARA*)

(**Above, left**) IJN Rear-Admiral Minoru Ota, commander of the Japanese naval forces defending the Oroku Peninsula. His experience was with naval artillery and SNLF troops, which Ota used effectively on New Georgia against the US Marines' 1st Raider Battalion (commanded by Colonel Harry Liversedge) at Enogai Inlet and Bairoko Harbour. From within his Naval Headquarters' underground bunker in the Oroku Peninsula, Ota committed suicide with a handgun on 13 June. (*Author's Collection*)

(**Left**) Lieutenant-General Mitsuru Ushijima, the IJA 32nd Army commander. Ushijima assumed command from an ailing Lieutenant-General Masao Watanabe, the formation's initial leader. Ushijima was known for his integrity, competence and respect for his subordinates. He was complemented by his COS, Lieutenant-General Cho, who was very aggressive and a martinet. Colonel Hirimichi Yahara, as IJA 32nd Army's senior operations officer, rounded out the triumvirate as the lone holdover from Watanabe's previous staff. (*Author's Collection*)

(**Above, right**) Some of the neatly attired Japanese officers and enlisted men that surrendered to US Tenth Army forces on the Motobu Peninsula. This scene contrasted that at naval headquarters' underground bunker in the Oroku Peninsula, where Rear-Admiral Ota and many of his subordinates committed suicide. (*NARA*)

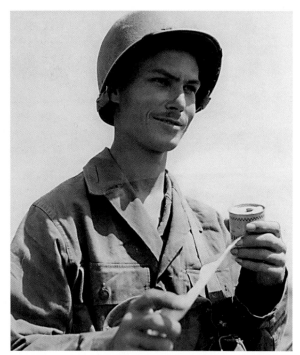 

(**Above, left**) PFC Desmond Doss, a twice Bronze Star-decorated combat medic (from action on Guam and Leyte), attached to the 2nd Platoon, Company B, 1st Battalion of the 77th Division's 307th Infantry Regiment, after early May's Maeda Escarpment battle (Hacksaw Ridge). The 307th Regiment had taken over the Maeda Escarpment part of the line from the 96th Division's 381st Regiment. Doss, a Seventh Day Adventist, refused to use a weapon as a conscientious objector. After horrific Japanese counter-attacks atop the escarpment against the battalion-strength elements of the 307th Regiment, Doss remained among his wounded comrades after the others had been driven off the height. Doss lowered scores of wounded over the escarpment's face via a rope litter and then approached the enemy caves to rescue some others. Doss was later given the Congressional Medal of Honor for his heroism, the only conscientious objector to receive this award during the war. Doss was wounded four times on Okinawa and was evacuated from the island on 21 May. The 307th Regiment's 1st Battalion lost eight company commanders in just thirty-six hours of combat. The 1st Battalion ascended the escarpment with scaling ladders and naval cargo nets on 29 April with a typical strength of 800 men. However, on 7 May, the battalion's remnants descended Hacksaw Ridge with only 324 soldiers. An estimated 3,000 Japanese troops were killed by the 77th Division during the Maeda Escarpment's week-long battle. Hacksaw Ridge temporally coincided with Ushijima's 4 May surprise counter-offensive to reclaim previous ground lost to the US Tenth Army. (*NARA*)

(**Above, right**) Leif Erickson of acting fame in his wartime service capacity as a US Navy combat photographer for Fleet Motion Picture Office. Here he is aboard a Landing Ship Medium (LSM) Rocket (R) launcher on night patrol off Green Beach 2 in early April. (*NARA*)

(**Opposite, above**) Ernie Pyle, War Correspondent (*third from left*), with Marines on 8 April, ten days before being shot by a Japanese soldier during the US 77th Infantry Division's fighting on Ie Shima. Pyle and a 77th Division regimental commander were at the front-lines, when their Jeep was driven into a ditch by enemy machine-gunfire. Moments later, Pyle was killed instantly while peering from their shelter. Pyle's grave at the 77th Division's cemetery on Ie Shima read: 'At this spot, the 77th Infantry Division lost a buddy, Ernie Pyle, 18th April 1945.' (*NARA*)

(**Opposite, below**) Lieutenant-Colonel William Kratich (*centre, wearing baseball hat*), a Marine Air Control operations officer, briefs pilots for their fighter-bomber attack on enemy positions. The sortie was to support Marine riflemen as they pressed their attack in southern Okinawa. (*USMC*)

(**Above**) Marine Corporal William C. Beall, a combat photographer, in the dorsal rear turret, designed to house a Browning 0.5-inch calibre machine-gun, of his Grumman TBF *Avenger* torpedo bomber after an aerial reconnaissance mission over southern Okinawa. His photograph reconnaissance sortie was escorted by Marine *Corsair* fighters. (*NARA*)

(**Opposite**) Lieutenant-Colonel Richard P. Ross, Jr, Commanding Officer 3rd Battalion, 1st Marines, scales a parapet at Shuri Castle to plant the 'Stars and Stripes' of the 1st Marine Division on the morning of 29 May. This particular flag was previously carried by the 1st Marine Division at Cape Gloucester and on Peleliu. Shuri Castle was captured by the 1st Battalion, 5th Marines (commanded by Lieutenant-Colonel Charles W. Shelburne). Major-General del Valle granted permission for a Marine assault company to storm the Japanese fortifications despite the fact that the castle itself was within the 77th Division's zone. This move created some consternation for Major-General Bruce, the Army division's commander, who was narrowly able to cancel a 77th planned artillery barrage of the castle. After the action, del Valle opined that the more prompt Marine capture of this important enemy strongpoint garnered tactical and morale gains sooner than the anticipated several more days of hard 77th Division fighting needed to take the position. (*NARA*)

(**Opposite, above**) The 77th Division American flag atop the 600-foot Iegusugu Mountain on the island of Ie Shima. The heaviest fighting occurred here during the island's assault from 16–21 April. (*Author's Collection*)

(**Above**) Lieutenant (j.g.) Thomas M. Davis, USNR, a South Carolinian, attaches a small CSA 'Stars and Bars' flag to a denuded tree at the beach-head. Davis was an assistant surgeon with the 1st Marine Division that landed on the right side of IIIAC assault beaches on D-Day. Similarly, when Captain Julian D. Dusenbury, another South Carolinian, of the 1st Battalion, 5th Marines, hoisted a CSA 'Stars and Bars' flag over Shuri Castle on 29 May to honour the legacy of that battle insignia, some concern was generated at Tenth Army HQ, although its commander, Lieutenant-General Buckner, was the son of Confederate general Simon Bolivar Buckner. (*NARA*)

(**Opposite, below**) Colonel Alan Shapley, the 4th Marines, 6th Division commander, points out objectives to his subordinate officers on 20 May. That month, the 6th Marine Division was fighting on the western side of Okinawa with objectives such as Sugar Loaf, Half Moon, Horseshoe Ridges, all north of the Asato River. (*USMC*)

(**Opposite, above**) A US Army 96th Division infantry patrol moves cautiously along open ground with a radioman with his Single Channel Radio (SCR)-536 'walkie-talkie' in the centre keeping contact with his commander. The SCR-536 had fifty channels and was utilised for infantry company-platoon communication. The patrol was advancing towards 'Big Apple Hill' near Yuza, just north of the IJA 24th Division's final redoubt, in early June. (*USAMHI*)

(**Opposite, below**) Corporal Robert Gard, 96th Division's 382nd Infantry Regiment, uses his SCR-536 'walkie-talkie' to stay in contact with his Company H headquarters during combat in mid-June in the southern part of Okinawa. (*USAMHI*)

(**Above**) US 96th Division infantrymen take cover behind an M4 tank during their advance in mid-June on the Yaeju-Dake Peak ('Big Apple Peak'), which was a 4-mile-long cliff rising to 290 feet from the adjoining valley floor. Another hill mass, the Yuza-Dake Peak, stood at the western end of the Japanese defence-line further to the south, which tapered westward into Kunishi Ridge in IIIAC sector. This was difficult terrain for armour as the ground was composed of soft clay, especially after the rainy season. (*USAMHI*)

(**Above**) An M4 flame-throwing tank of the 731st TB projects flame onto enemy positions on the Maeda Escarpment. US 96th Division infantrymen were providing protection for their tanks as suicidal Japanese troops often rushed out of their concealed locales to attach explosive satchels to the American armour for quick detonation. The Maeda Escarpment, described as 'a huge, forbidding, sheer cliff', was a part of the Urasoe-Mura Escarpment in the 96th Division's zone. The attack against the Maeda Escarpment was launched on 26 April by the 381st Infantry Regiment, which had to initially scale the height before combating concealed enemy positions on the crest and reverse slope of the prominence. At Hills 150 and 152 to the east of the escarpment, tanks and armoured flame-throwers, accompanying the 96th's 383rd Infantry Regiment, were able to move to the edge of Maeda and wreaked havoc on exposed IJA infantrymen there. However, the IJA 24th Division, north-east of Shuri, bolstered the enemy resistance, limiting the 96th Division's gains to just yards. Due to American losses, the 77th Division's 306th and 307th Infantry Regiments took over the Maeda Escarpment part of the line from the 96th Division on 29 April. Attesting to the ferocity of combat, the 381st Infantry Regiment was reduced to 40 per cent combat efficiency, suffering over 1,000 casualties. (*NARA*)

(**Opposite**) Army PFC James Clark from the 77th Division's 305th Infantry Regiment loads an ammunition belt into his Browning M1917 0.3-inch calibre water-cooled MMG. Prior to the *Iceberg* landings at Hagushi on 1 April, the 1st and 3rd Battalions of the 305th assaulted Zamami and Aka Shima islands in the Kerama Retto on 26 March. The Kerama Retto was of little logistical value. However, it threatened the main Okinawa invasion as evidenced by the 350 Japanese suicide boats of a sea-raiding squadron destroyed by the 77th Division's units shortly after landing. The Kerama Retto's islands were defended by about 1,000 enemy troops. (*USAMHI*)

(**Opposite, above**) Soldiers of the US 7th Division's 32nd Infantry Regiment search surrendering enemy soldiers emerging from a cave. After landing at Hagushi on L-Day, the 32nd Regiment moved all three of its battalions southward along Nakagusuku Bay. After moving almost 3 miles unopposed, the 32nd began to receive some Japanese artillery fire, a sign that combat was to be soon enjoined despite an uneventful amphibious landing. (*USAMHI*)

(**Above**) Soldiers from Company B of the US 7th Division's 184th Infantry Regiment inspect the remnants of a Japanese gun emplacement. On 5 April, the 184th advanced through Arakachi and then their movement was halted by heavy and accurate fire from a rocky crest located about a half-mile south-west of the town. Company B assaulted the hill that day, but its attack was repulsed. The reduction of this enemy artillery position, termed the 'Pinnacle' after a thin coral spike that rose 30 feet above the 450-foot ridge, was defended by an HQ company of the IJA 14th Independent Infantry Battalion. The 184th Regiment's Company C was required to support the attack on the 'Pinnacle' the next day. (*USAMHI*)

(**Opposite, below**) An assault unit of the 1st Marine Division observes the effects of white phosphorus artillery shelling before their attack on Shuri Heights commenced on 11 May. The key Japanese positions were Dakeshi and Wana Ridges, Wana Draw, and the towns of Dakeshi and Wana, all of which protected Shuri on the north-west. By 10 May, the Americans were still short of the Tenth Army objective line to launch its general offensive. The naval commanders exhorted Buckner's forces to advance as there were heavy ship losses to *kamikaze* attacks. (*NARA*)

(**Opposite, above**) A trio of 6th Division Marines from 2nd Platoon, Company C, 1st Battalion, 22nd Marines take cover behind a cluster of trees as they exchange rifle fire and grenade-throwing with the enemy to their front in June. The Marines to the left and in the centre have their characteristic KA-BAR (derived from the manufacturer Ka-Bar Knives, Inc. of Olean, New York) knife attached to their webbing. The blade was 7 inches in length and weighed 4lb. In November 1942, the KA-BAR knife replaced the M1917 Stilettos (also known as Mk I Dagger) issued during the early months of the war as they had a longer blade with a non-reflective finish as well as fuller leather handle for easy gripping. These knives were later designated USMC Mk 2 combat knife, Fighting Utility. (*NARA*)

(**Above**) Marine PFC Leo Brady grins and flashes the 'OK' finger signal after 17 of his 20 105mm M7 HMC rounds hit their target. The characteristic 'pulpit'-shaped turret ring for the M7 armoured vehicle's Browning 0.50-inch calibre HMG is seen (*right*). A Browning 0.30-inch calibre LMG is to the left. (*NARA*)

(**Opposite, below**) Marine PFC Joseph Garrity fires a jet of flame at enemy snipers concealed in tombs and caves at a reverse slope base of an Okinawan ridge on 16 May. Each Marine rifle squad was issued with a flame-thrower. (*NARA*)

(**Above**) Marine Corporal Paul Robinson lights the fuse of an explosive satchel with his cigarette just prior to throwing it into a cave on Hill 69 on 12 June. On 10 June, the 1st Marine Division's 1st and 7th Marines advanced abreast of one another for their attack on Kunishi Ridge, on Okinawa's southern tip. A 1st Marines' battalion lost over a hundred men killed or wounded to take a small hill west of Yuza town. That same day, the 7th Marines fought for a long ridge at the northern edge of Tera. On 11 June, Hill 69, west of Ozato, was attacked against determined enemy opposition from caves such as this one. (*NARA*)

(**Opposite, above**) Thirty-one 6th Division Marines of L Company, 3rd Battalion, 22nd Marines together on 25 June with some combat souvenirs obtained at a very steep price. These were the surviving Marines out of 240 who landed on 1 April at Hagushi. Twenty-four of the thirty-one were previously wounded in combat and returned to active duty. (*NARA*)

(**Opposite, below**) A 1st Division Marine patrol with an SB in the lead advances at double pace across an open field on 10 May towards Shuri Heights as part of the Tenth Army offensive. A dead Marine, killed by a mortar blast, is shown (*foreground*). (*NARA*)

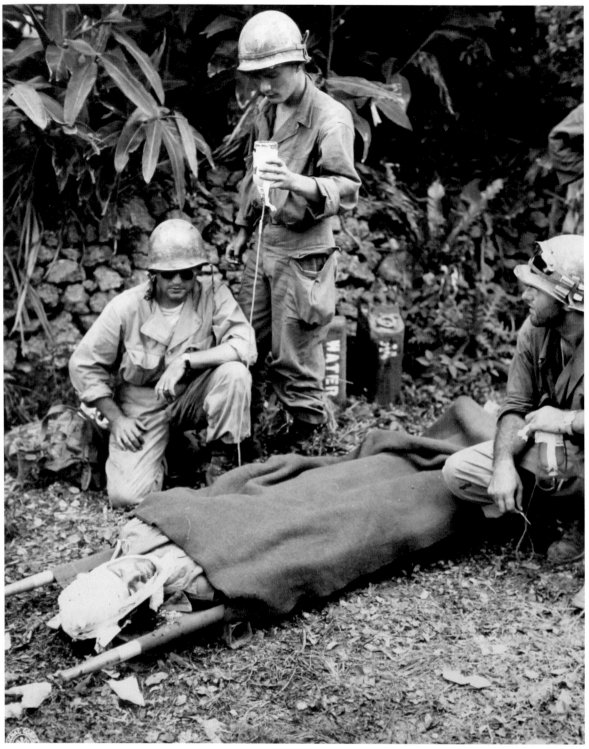

US Army Captain James Barron (on stretcher) receives a plasma infusion administered by combat medics. Barron was wounded by a Japanese sniper on 4 April. (*USAMHI*)

Two Navy corpsmen carry a wounded Marine on a stretcher while under direct enemy observation and fire on 12 June during the Battle for Kunishi Ridge, where the IJA 24th Division fought off a US 96th Division infantry regiment and elements of the 1st Marine Division from 12–17 June. Over 140 men from two battalions of the 7th Marines were casualties with the seriously wounded brought to the rear by SBs and tanks. *(NARA)*

A pair of 'walking wounded' with non-life-threatening injuries return to the rear for further aid during April's combat. US Navy Pharmacist Mate 3rd Class Vernon Martin (*front*) with Private First-Class Robert Schlosser behind him. (*NARA*)

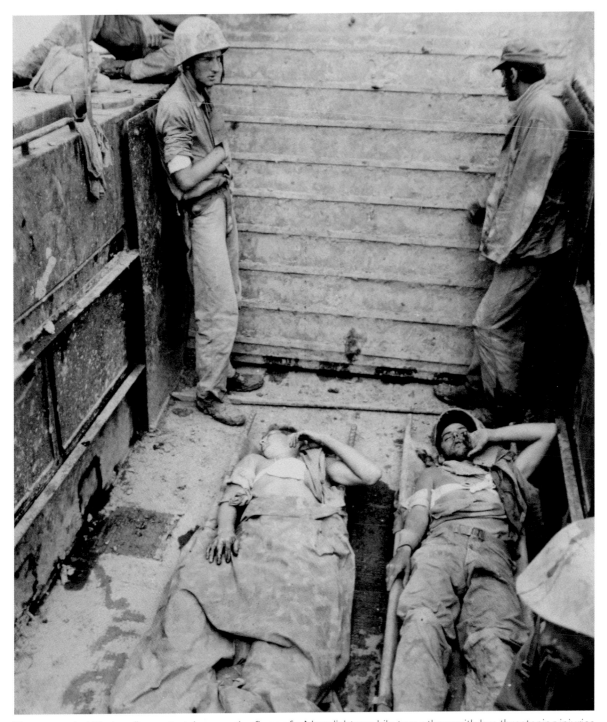

Two wounded Marines lie on stretchers on the floor of a Navy lighter while two others with less threatening injuries stand during evacuation to a hospital ship off the Hagushi beaches. Despite Red Cross markings, hospital ships were subjected to *kamikaze* attacks. (*NARA*)

A wounded sailor is transported on a litter via a rope line from the burning carrier USS *Bunker Hill* to the USS *Wilkes-Barre*, a Cleveland-class light cruiser, after a devastating *kamikaze* attack on the former vessel. The *Bunker Hill*, an *Essex*-class carrier, was struck by two *kamikazes* in quick succession, turning it into an inferno on the morning of 11 May. A Mitsubishi A6M Zero Japanese fighter dropped a 500lb bomb that penetrated the flight deck and exited the ship before exploding. However, that Zero crashed into the flight deck amid fuelled planes loaded with ammunition. Within a minute a second Zero dropped another 500lb bomb and crashed into the flight deck near the carrier's 'island'. This second bomb penetrated the flight deck and exploded in the pilots' ready room, killing twenty-two members of VF-84. Subsequent aviation fuel fires and ammunition explosions ensued. Casualties exceeded 600, including about 350 sailors and officers confirmed killed and almost fifty missing. The *Bunker Hill* was the flagship of Vice-Admiral Mitscher. His COS, Commodore Burke, and the admiral's staff were also on the vessel. Three officers and nine sailors from Mitscher's staff were casualties. The *Wilkes-Barre* came alongside the burning *Bunker Hill* and, in addition to transferring fire-fighting and rescue gear, began the arduous task of taking aboard the carrier's injured and dying. Both the US Navy and the Royal Navy suffered horrific losses to the successive waves of *kamikaze* attacks during the eighty-two-day campaign. There was a total of thirty-six American ships sunk and 368 damaged, with more than 10 per cent of the latter vessels being scrapped. The Royal Navy's British Carrier Force (TF 57) suffered four ships damaged with almost 150 seamen killed or wounded during the enemy aerial attacks. (*NARA*)

A Navy corpsman starts an intravenous for a wounded Marine in a cave converted into a temporary hospital near Naha's front-lines. In addition to medical supplies in a box next to the corpsman, a container labelled 'SPOTLIGHT' is visible for cave illumination. (*NARA*)

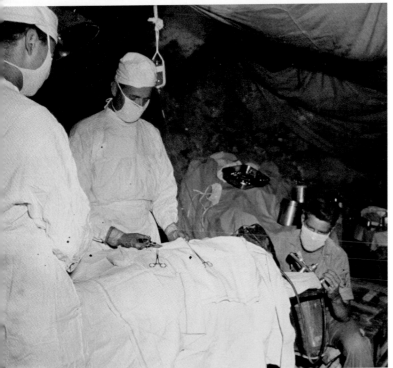

The adage 'Medicine is where you find it' is apt for this photograph, as Navy surgeons perform an operation from within an operating room inside a large tent in a Okinawan rear echelon area. A corpsman to the right administers anaesthesia outside of the surgeons' sterile field with plasma being infused above the centre surgeon's head. (*NARA*)

153

(**Above**) A quartet of emaciated Japanese soldiers carry one of their injured under a 2nd Battalion, 29th Marines' escort after surrendering on 19 June, days before enemy resistance ceased. Note that the enemy soldiers are stripped to a minimum of clothing to prevent them from hiding weapons and explosives, which was a common suicidal tactic after capture. *(NARA)*

(**Opposite, above left**) Three enemy combatants stand beside one another after their capture. The two to the left are teenage Japanese soldiers while the one on the right is a Korean labourer, exhibiting a marked disparity in height despite his relative young age. *(NARA)*

(**Opposite, above right**) A trio of Japanese soldiers behind the wire of a temporary detention facility on 20 June after surrendering. The elderly man to the left was 75 years old, while the centre and right teenage combatants were 16 and 15 years old, respectively. All three are wearing the distinctive split-toe, lightweight *Tabi* boot, which was designed to give them better grip on difficult terrain or when climbing walls or trees. *(USAMHI)*

(**Opposite, below**) A Japanese soldier lies dead next to a disabled American tank in May. He was trying to infiltrate American lines dressed in a captured Marine uniform and was most likely on a suicide mission to detonate explosives once within them. *(NARA)*

(**Above**) A member of the 4th Marines, 6th Division carefully peers into a rock crevice holding his M1 Garand semi-automatic rifle, on 16 April. Moments before, he had killed a Japanese sniper with a hand-grenade. The Japanese infantryman's order was to maximally delay the Americans' advance while inflicting the most casualties on the Tenth Army, as the *kamikazes* wreaked havoc with the US Navy offshore. (*NARA*)

(**Opposite, above**) The charred remains of a Japanese artilleryman lie next to the smouldering ruins of a 47mm AT gun out in the open that was destroyed by an American flame-throwing tank. Such was the suicidal resistance offered by Japanese soldiers on Okinawa that typified the combat across the Pacific. (*NARA*)

(**Opposite, below**) African-Americans from the 11th Marine Depot Company move through the sand at Peleliu in mid-September 1944, where they served as SBs for the 7th Marines, 1st Division at the beach-head. Seventeen men from this company were wounded during the island's combat and received commendation letters from the 1st Marine Division commander, Major-General William H. Rupertus. Breaking a 167-year interval, the Marine Corps began enlisting African-Americans on 1 June 1942 following an executive order by President Roosevelt. Training for 1,200 volunteers soon commenced for the members of the 51st Composite Defence Battalion at Camp Lejeune's Montford Point at New River, North Carolina. (*NARA*)

Marine PFC Luther Woodward of the 4th Ammunition Company admires his Bronze Star for 'bravery, initiative and battle-cunning' during combat on Guam in January 1945. The award was upgraded to a Silver Star on 17 April 1945. Approximately 19,000 African-Americans served as Marines during the war, with over 11,000 in the Pacific in units such as the 51st and 52nd Defence Battalions, the Stewards Branch, as well as Ammunition and Depot Companies. On 3 April, Ammunition and Depot Companies landed on Okinawa to support the 1st and 6th Marine Divisions. Over 2,000 African-American Marines participated in this last battle of the Pacific War. (NARA)

Marines from the Navajo tribe, Corporal Henry Bake and PFC George Kirk with their radio set on Bougainville in late 1943. These Native Americans transmitted radio messages in a code based on the Navajo language, which was indecipherable to the Japanese. On Iwo Jima, the 'code-talkers' transmitted 800 radio messages within the first forty-eight hours of that island's invasion without an error. (NARA)

Navajo 'code talker' Carl Nelson Gorman scans the front-lines for Japanese movements on Saipan in late July 1944. From 1942 to 1945, over 400 'code-talkers' participated in all Marine divisions and specialised units' assaults in the Pacific. The war correspondent Ernie Pyle reported that on the eve of the Okinawa invasion, the Navajos performed a sacred dance asking for divine blessings and protection for their 1st Marine Division's landings at Hagushi. (NARA)

Chapter Four

US Tenth Army's Amphibious Assault on Okinawa

The Kerama Retto islands, approximately 15 miles west of Okinawa, were the initial Ryukyus' target for the Allies and were assaulted by battalions of the US 77th Division's 305th, 306th and 307th Infantry Regiments, veterans of the Leyte campaign, on 26–27 March. The strategic goal was securing a sea-plane base and fleet anchorage to support *Iceberg's* main landings on 1 April. The 77th Division's battalions met little opposition. Keise Shima's seizure by the US 420th Field Artillery Group, 11 miles south-west of the main invasion's Hagushi assault beaches, occurred on 31 March after initial Marine reconnaissance five days earlier. This occupation was to provide artillery support for the *Iceberg* landings. Awara Shima at the Kerama Retto's eastern end was launched by the Marine Reconnaissance Battalion from Keise Shima.

An intense naval and aerial bombardment preceded L-Day's Okinawa amphibious invasion on 1 April (Easter Sunday or April Fool's Day). LCI (Gun) vessels, mounting five 4.5-inch calibre guns and Mk 7 rocket launchers (with twelve HE rockets each), led the assault waves for their 4,000-yard run-in to the Hagushi beaches. These modified LCI craft fired mortars and 40mm guns onto a pre-arranged target square up to 1,000 yards inland. At the coral reef, these ships turned off as unescorted armoured amtracs (LVT (A)s) headed to the beaches. The LVT(A)s fired their 75mm Howitzers directly ahead of them at suspected enemy positions. Hundreds of troop-carrying LVTs, five to seven waves deep, followed the LVT(A)s. As naval bombardment lifted, circling carrier-borne aircraft commenced bombing and strafing runs at suspected Japanese beach positions.

At 0830hrs, the initial assault waves reached their assigned zones. IIIAC, comprising the 6th and 1st Marines Divisions, was the left half of Tenth Army's assault to the south-west of Nagahama. The 22nd and 4th Marines, 6th Division landed at *Green* 1 and 2 beaches as well as *Red* 1, 2 and 3 beaches, respectively. The 4th Marines were directly opposite the Yontan Airfield. The 7th and 5th Marines of the 1st Division landed at *Blue* 1 and 2 as well as *Yellow* 1 and 2 beaches, respectively. The 7th Marines were opposite Irammiya, while the 5th Marines landed at Hagushi. The 29th Marines, 6th Division were IIIAC's floating reserve.

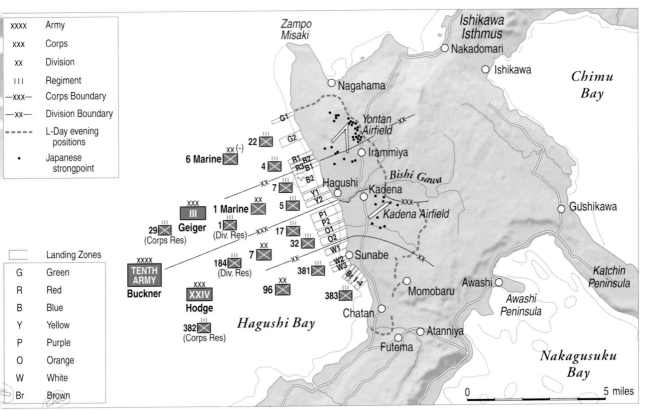

Landing (L)-Day: Invasion of Okinawa on 1 April 1945. At 0830hrs, Tenth Army's initial assault waves reached their assigned Hagushi beach zones. The *Bishi Gawa* separated the Marines' IIIAC (6th and 1st Marines Divisions) assault zone on the left from the army's XXIV Corps (7th and 96th Divisions) on the right half of the beach frontage between the inland locales of Nagahama and Chatan to the north and south, respectively. The 22nd and 4th Marines of the 6th Division landed at Green 1 and 2 beaches as well as Red 1, 2 and 3 beaches, respectively. The 4th Marines were directly opposite the Yontan Airfield. The 7th and 5th Marines of the 1st Division landed at Blue 1 and 2 as well as Yellow 1 and 2 beaches, respectively. The 7th Marines were opposite the inland locale of Irammiya, while the 5th Marines landed in front of Hagushi.

Eight XXIV Corps battalions landed south of the *Bishi Gawa* in six successive waves of LVT (A)s. The 7th Division's 17th Infantry Regiment landed at Purple 1 and 2 beaches opposite the Kadena Airfield inland, while the 32nd Infantry Regiment assaulted Orange 1 and 2 beaches. On the right flank of the Tenth Army, the 96th Division's 381st Infantry Regiment landed at White 1, 2 and 3 beaches opposite the locale of Sunabe, while that division's 383rd Infantry Regiment assaulted the beach frontage on a northerly tangent at Brown 1, 2, 3 and 4 beaches just to the north-west of Chatan.

The assault force faced light resistance with almost no landing-beach mines or obstacles as over 16,000 troops landed within L-Day's first hour. On 1 April, there were only twenty-eight men killed, 104 wounded and twenty-seven missing. Offshore, unloading activity was brisk from the transports into landing craft and amtracs. *(Meridian Mapping)*

The *Bishi Gawa*, with the waterway's mouth just to the south of Hagushi, separated the IIIAC assault zone from Tenth Army's XXIV Corps beach frontage. Despite some reef and Japanese mortar-fire, the eight XXIV Corps battalions landed south of the *Bishi Gawa* in six successive waves of LVT(A)s. The Army's 7th Division's 17th Infantry Regiment landed at Purple 1 and 2 beaches opposite the Kadena Airfield inland, while the 32nd Infantry Regiment assaulted Orange 1 and 2 beaches. On the right flank, the 96th Division's 381st Infantry Regiment landed at White 1, 2 and 3 beaches opposite the locale of Sunabe, while that division's 383rd Infantry Regiment assaulted the beach frontage on a northerly tangent at Brown 1, 2, 3 and 4 beaches just north-west of Chatan.

In the XXIV Corps zone, a sea-wall was breached by naval gunfire and army combat engineers in the initial waves. These openings in the sea-wall provided beach exits for 4.2-inch mortar-equipped DUKWs and M4 tanks to move inland and fan out to protect XXIV Corps' flanks.

The Tenth Army's assaulting divisions faced light resistance with few beach mines or obstacles as over 16,000 assault troops arrived within L-Day's first hour. Offshore of the Hagushi beaches, vigorous unloading activity from the transports into landing craft and amtracs continued. In all, Tenth Army suffered twenty-eight men killed, 104 wounded and twenty-seven missing as Ushijima intended to primarily defend the southern half of Okinawa and not mount resistance to the Hagushi landings.

The 7th Division, after seizing Kadena airfield, was to advance in tandem with the 1st Marine Division to Okinawa's east coast to bisect the island. The 96th Division was tasked with seizing the high ground above the beaches and then move south down the coast road to capture the bridges in the vicinity of Chatan and secure Tenth Army's southern flank.

The Americans conducted a feint landing with the Demonstration Group (2nd Marine Division) off Minatoga on Okinawa's east coast to the Chinen Peninsula's south. This action diverted some Japanese air defence from the Hagushi fleet. Japanese *kamikazes*, attacking some of the transports of the Demonstration Group, produced the first casualties of Operation *Iceberg*.

(**Opposite, above**) The USS *Idaho*, a New Mexico-class battleship launched in 1917, fires a salvo with twelve 14-inch guns at Japanese positions on Okinawa as landing craft converge for the several thousand-yard run-in to the Hagushi beaches on 1 April. The *Idaho* had participated in the amphibious operations against the Gilbert, Marshall and Philippine Islands as well as at Peleliu and Iwo Jima. *(NARA)*

(**Opposite, below**) LSM (Rocket)-188 vessels fire a barrage of 5-inch rockets against enemy positions within the Okinawa beach-head on 1 April. The LSM (Rocket) had a crew of five officers and seventy-six enlisted sailors manning seventy-five four-rail topside Mk 36 rocket launchers along with one 5-inch calibre naval gun aft and an assortment of 20mm and 40mm AA guns. These vessels were commissioned in November–December 1944 after rapid construction at South Carolina's Charleston Navy Yard. LSM(R)-190, 194 and 195 were sunk by Japanese *kamikaze* planes while on picket duty on 3–4 May, with many casualties incurred. *(NARA)*

(**Above**) A US Navy Grumman F4F Wildcat fighter takes off from a fast carrier in support of Tenth Army landings at the Hagushi beaches on 1 April. The single-seat fighter/fighter-bomber entered service after the Japanese attack on Pearl Harbor in December 1941 and remained in production throughout the war. With a maximum speed of just over 300mph, the Wildcat was powerful with six 0.5-inch Browning HMGs in the wings and could carry a 200lb external bomb. (*NARA*)

(**Opposite, above**) Marines of IIIAC clamber down chain and wooden rung ladders of a transport into a LCVP (also called a 'Higgins Boat') on 1 April. These landing craft were designed by the American boat builder Andrew Higgins, based on shallow-draft vessels used in Louisiana swamps and marshes. Thirty-six assault troops plus a crew of four could be accommodated by the vessel and it was able to move to shore at 9 knots. The LCVP was also able to transport a Jeep and a twelve-man squad or 8,000lb of cargo. (*NARA*)

(**Opposite, below**) The presence of coral reef prevented the movement of LCVPs to the shoreline's sand, where the assault troops could exit the craft by running down the boat's anchored bow ramp. So, assaulting Marines are shown transferring from a LCVP to a LVT (4) in order to facilitate movement across the reef's fringe at some places at the Hagushi beach-head. (*NARA*)

A US Navy signalman waves control craft pennants from aboard an LCVP (*foreground*) to facilitate the grouping of other troop-laden LCVPs and LVTs for the several thousand-yard run-in to the beaches. A destroyer, the USS *Richard P. Leary*, provides 5-inch naval gun support for the amphibious craft heading ashore. (*NARA*)

A wave of LVT (Armoured) craft moves towards shore. The initial wave contained 28 of these 'amtanks' firing their 75mm Howitzers at suspected Japanese positions at the shoreline before the troop-laden vessels arrived. (*USMC*)

Riflemen from the 2nd Battalion, 22nd Marines of the 6th Marine Division, which comprised the extreme left flank of Tenth Army at Green Beach 1, emerge down the ramp from the rear of a LVT 4 to commence the assault on the Hagushi beaches on 1 April. The Marine (*foreground*) is carrying a Thompson 0.45-inch calibre sub-machine-gun, while the one in the rear is the squad's flame-thrower armed with his 0.45-inch calibre 1911 semi-automatic pistol holstered on his right hip. Another LVT4 (*background*) was armed with a pair of shielded 0.5-inch calibre HMGs. (*USMC*)

Riflemen from the 1st Battalion, 7th Marines, 1st Division scale Blue Beach 2's sea-wall on 1 April. The Marines carried an assortment of infantry weapons, including an M1 Garand semi-automatic rifle (*left*) and a Winchester M12 combat shotgun (*centre*). The M12 had a woven canvas sling and could mount a bayonet. The M12 also featured a shorter barrel with a perforated sleeve as a heat shield for the shooter's hand while firing. The rugged and reliable shotgun was extremely effective at close ranges in and around bunkers and trenches. (*NARA*)

(**Opposite, above**) Riflemen from the 2nd Battalion, 7th Marines of the 1st Division ascend a section of sea-wall breached by naval gunfire on 1 April. This battalion's Marines comprised the left flank of the division at Blue 1 and 2 landing beaches. (*NARA*)

(**Above**) An LVT heads to shore amid other non-tracked landing craft with soldiers of the 7th Division on 1 April. This XXIV Corps division assaulted frontage comprising two Purple and two Orange landing beaches located to the right of the 1st Marine Division. (*Author's Collection*)

(**Opposite, below**) Soldiers of the 96th Division climb over the front of a landing craft at one of the three White landing beaches comprising the southern flank of the Tenth Army invasion on 1 April. After disembarking from the craft, the soldiers had to climb the sea-wall using a scaling ladder propped against it. The landing craft was protected by two shielded 0.50-inch calibre HMGs. (*NARA*)

(**Opposite, above**) Marines wade ashore onto one of the two IIIAC sectors on 1 April. Only sporadic enemy artillery and mortar rounds were fired at the assault troops as the Marines moved to the beach, and then beyond the sea-wall and some elevated terrain immediately inland. (*NARA*)

(**Opposite, below**) Marines, probably regimental support troops, carry supplies from transports close to the shoreline later in the day on 1 April. As shown, at low tide, the unloading of heavier equipment was hampered and had to be manhandled. Japanese resistance was not present at Yontan and Kadena airfields as enemy service troops there were untrained for any organised combat. (*NARA*)

(**Above**) With the Okinawa landings unopposed, a feared repetition of the bloody assaults at Iwo Jima and Peleliu was averted. Within the initial few hours after the landings commenced, 50,000 American troops were ashore. Assault craft, larger transports and smaller warships are shown offshore (*background*). By mid-afternoon of 1 April, some divisional artillery and support elements commenced landing at the secure beach-head. (*NARA*)

Marines leisurely study maps to prepare for the move inland at an IIIAC landing beach's sea-wall. Elements of the 4th Marines, 6th Division were to be in position at the southern end of the Yontan Airfield by late morning of L-Day. Soldiers of the army's 7th Division's 17th Infantry Regiment were also successful at reaching Kadena Airfield at a similar time. (*NARA*)

A Marine casualty on L-Day is tended by a Navy corpsman near the assault beach. Without fanatical Japanese beach-head resistance that characterised many Pacific island amphibious attacks, Tenth Army casualties were extremely light. (*NARA*)

Marines march in single-file inland as a plethora of landing craft and transports, such as LST 1000, lay close to shore. By 1 April's end, an 8.5-mile-long beach-head frontage was established and up to 3 miles deep. By L-Day+1, the flanks of IIIAC to the north and XXIV south of the *Bishi Gawa* were made. (*NARA*)

Marine infantrymen with full gear march inland behind an LVT 4 on 1 April. A Marine M4 medium tank (*right*) was probably landed by a LCM or LST. (*NARA*)

Elements of 4th Marines, 6th Division unload supplies from an LVT 4 and sequester them under the camouflage netting of a destroyed Japanese fighter at Yontan Airfield on L-Day. The LVT 4 was armed with two shielded 0.5-inch calibre HMGs. (*NARA*)

Marine Vought F4U Corsair fighter-bombers taxiing at Yontan Airfield. These aircraft provided close support for Marine units that were beginning to encounter stiffer Japanese resistance from inland fortifications. Armed with bombs, rockets and six fixed 0.5-inch calibre wing machine-guns, the Corsairs were formidable in their ground-attack role. Yontan Airfield was captured by 6th Division Marines on L-Day. Navy planners did not expect to possess the airfield until L-Day+3. (NARA)

As Marines moved inland on 1 April, a US Navy Grumman TBF Avenger (background) was flying a bombing sortie as close support. In addition to its forward and rearward-firing machine-guns, the Avenger was able to carry up to 2,500lb as either a bomb- or rocket-load when not carrying its torpedoes. (NARA)

(**Above**) The Operation *Iceberg* invasion fleet spans Okinawa's offshore waters as it unloads supplies and ordnance from a variety of shallow-draft transports. These vessels were to be ripe targets for the Japanese *kamikaze* pilots, along with carriers and picket vessels. Massed *kamikaze* attacks were more successful and wrought greater destruction against the Allies than the IJA 32nd Army's early May counter-offensive. (*Author's Collection*)

(**Opposite, above**) American sailors man a twin 40mm Bofors AA gun on an attack transport. This versatile weapon, used in single, twin or quad configurations, was vital for the Navy's defence against relentless *kamikaze* aerial assaults. Numerous racks of four-round 40 mm shells are shown (*left*). (*NARA*)

(**Opposite, below**) *Kamikaze* pilots tighten their *hachimaki* over their headgear before starting a one-way mission against Allied surface ships. The suicide mission was a duty-bound one, influenced by *bushido*, the Japanese warrior's code of conduct that served as a Buddhist or spiritual foundation for bravery and conscience. Their attack fervour was rooted in a belief of 'life through death'. (*Author's Collection*)

A dramatic photograph taken by Lieutenant-Commander Earl Colgrove, USNR, of the Naval Aviation Photographic Unit, led by Commander Edward Steichen. It vividly shows a *kamikaze* fighter, afire from AA gunfire, just before it crashed into a American fast carrier. Against Allied carriers, the aiming point for a *kamikaze* pilot was the central elevator with the next best target the fore or aft elevator. Against other Allied surface vessels, the bridge was the best target. Against destroyers and other smaller 'picket' ships, which suffered grievous losses to the *kamikaze* onslaught, a hit with either a 500lb bomb or with the Japanese aircraft itself between the bridge and the ship's centre usually crippled the vessel. The Allies had too many aircraft carriers and the Japanese too few available aircraft to deter the fleet's offshore support for the Tenth Army ground on Okinawa. (*NARA*)

The HMS *Formidable* of the Royal Navy's British Pacific Fleet attached to Task Force 57 ablaze after the aircraft carrier was attacked during a 4 May *kamikaze* assault. HMS *Formidable* was an Illustrious-class aircraft carrier that campaigned throughout the entire war after its 1940 completion. In the Pacific, it carried TBF Avengers, Corsairs and Hellcats. A Japanese 'Zeke' fighter emerged at 3,000 feet astern of the carrier, which completely surprised the ship expecting recovery of its combat air patrol. With only accompanying destroyers available to supplement the carrier's AA guns, the *kamikaze* fighter attacked the ship from the starboard quarter. Although ablaze, the Japanese pilot released his bomb from 700 feet before crashing into the armoured flight deck. Sheets of flame billowed from the carrier's island. (*Author's Collection*)

British seamen aboard the Royal Navy's HMS *Formidable* combat fires on the flight deck as smoke billows from the carrier's island after a 4 May *kamikaze* attack. Eight crewmen died with another fifty-five injured. However, the veteran carrier survived the war. (*Author's Collection*)

Chapter Five

Tenth Army Advance and the Protracted Conquest of Okinawa

Offshore island assaults

To ensure the Tenth Army's flanks and the Allied offshore supply efforts, the Eastern Islands guarding the Nakagusuku and Chimu Bays as well as Ie Shima (opposite the Motobu Peninsula) had to be secured. On 6 April, Marine reconnaissance troops landed on Tsugen Shima and, after meeting intense Japanese mortar and machine-gunfire, the American force withdrew. On 10 April, the 3rd Battalion, 105th Infantry Regiment, 27th Division landed on Tsugen Shima. In over a day of harsh combat the island was captured at a cost of ninety-four American casualties (including eleven killed in action), while over 200 Japanese were killed with no prisoners taken. On 7 April, other 27th Division units reconnoitred the Eastern Islands and found them devoid of Japanese troops. Nakagusuku Bay was now open to Vice-Admiral Turner's transports for re-supply of the XXIV Corps troops on Okinawa's eastern coast.

The next offshore island amphibious assault (under Rear-Admiral Reifsnider) at Ie Shima was conducted by elements of the US 77th Division on 16 April. Previously, this division had successfully assaulted Kerama Retto before *Iceberg* was launched. Prior to the 77th's attack on Ie Shima, a Marine Reconnaissance battalion occupied Minna Shima, 3 miles to the south-east. After the unopposed Marine seizure, the 77th's artillery was landed for gunfire support for the Ie Shima invasion.

Japanese opposition on Ie Shima landings was initially light. However, over the next six days the enemy fought from caves and tombs in, at times, vicious hand-to-hand combat. The main Japanese position atop the heights of Iegusugu Yama overlooking the village of Ie Shima was defended by 7,000 enemy troops. Locales such as 'Bloody Ridge' and 'Government House' were seized on 20 April by a 77th Division bayonet and grenade attack. After securing the island on 21 April, the 77th Division had incurred over 1,100 casualties, including 239 killed in action. One of the Ie Shima American casualties was War Correspondent Ernie Pyle, who was killed on 18 April

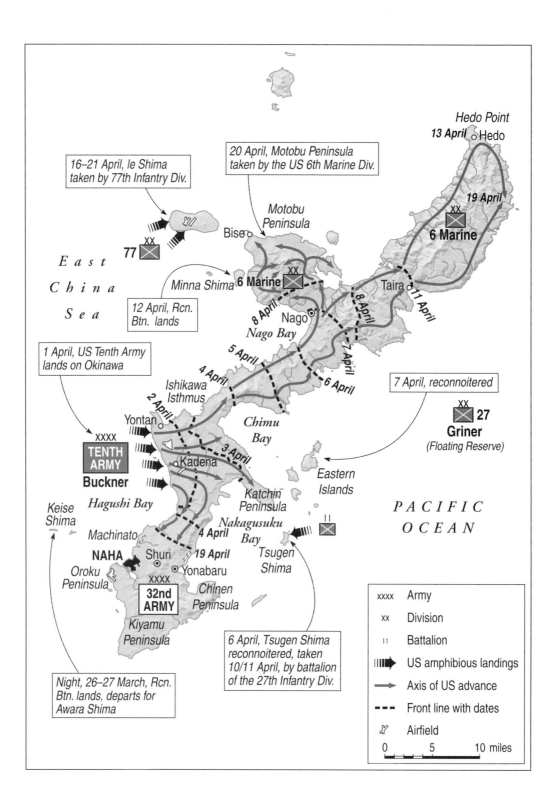

16–21 April, Ie Shima taken by 77th Infantry Div.

20 April, Motobu Peninsula taken by the US 6th Marine Div.

Hedo Point
13 April ○ Hedo

19 April

XX
6 Marine

East
China
Sea

Motobu Peninsula

Bise ○

XX
77

Minna Shima ● XX **6 Marine**

12 April, Rcn. Btn. lands

8 April

Nago ○

Taira ○

11 April

8 April

Nago Bay

1 April, US Tenth Army lands on Okinawa

5 April

4 April

Ishikawa Isthmus

2 April

Yontan ○

XXXX
TENTH ARMY
Buckner

Chimu Bay

Kadena ○

3 April

Keise Shima

Hagushi Bay

Machinato

NAHA

Oroku Peninsula

Shuri ◎

XXXX
32nd ARMY

Kiyamu Peninsula

7 April

6 April

7 April, reconnoitered

XX
27
Griner
(Floating Reserve)

Katchin Peninsula

Eastern Islands

PACIFIC OCEAN

Nakagusuku Bay

○ Yonabaru

Chinen Peninsula

4 April

19 April

II
XX

Tsugen Shima

Night, 26–27 March, Rcn. Btn. lands, departs for Awara Shima

6 April, Tsugen Shima reconnoitered, taken 10/11 April, by battalion of the 27th Infantry Div.

xxxx	Army
xx	Division
II	Battalion
⟶	US amphibious landings
→	Axis of US advance
- - -	Front line with dates
✈	Airfield

0   5   10 miles

by an enemy sniper's bullet to his head. After this hard-fought action, the 77th Division was transported back to Okinawa to bolster the XXIV Corps' drive to the south.

Opening inland movements

Iceberg's main unopposed Hagushi amphibious landings progressed with swift XXIV Corps movements inland under favourable weather. By 2 April's midday, the 7th Division's 17th Infantry Regiment reached the heights above Nakagusuku Bay, having crossed to Okinawa's east coast from south of the Kadena Airfield. Okinawa was bisected with Japanese forces separated into northern and southern sectors. Just to the south, the 7th Division's 32nd Infantry Regiment moved inland after an armoured reduction of an enemy fortified position. The 96th Division, on Tenth Army's right flank, made slow progress early on 2 April near Shido as heavily forested ridges, empty caves and dugouts along with mine-laden rough trails were obstacles.

To the north, elements of the 29th Marines, 6th Division cleared Zampo Misaki on the peninsula to the landing beaches' north-west. The 6th Division's 4th Marines advanced through rugged terrain, 'honeycombed' with many caves and met increasing Japanese resistance on L-Day+1. By sunset of 2 April, the 6th Marine Division's left flank was at the base of the Ishikawa Isthmus ahead of schedule. The 7th and 5th Marines, 1st Division crossed the island's centre against only local Japanese resistance and were poised to push south into the Katchin Peninsula on Okinawa's eastern coast. Elements of the 1st Marine Division even took the small island of Yabuchi Shima at the tip of the Katchin Peninsula by 6 April. In these actions, IIIAC Marines killed over 900 local Japanese defenders, while capturing twenty-six.

With these early gains, a several mile-wide gap existed between IIIAC and XXIV Corps that was closed by the 7th Division's reserve, the 184th Infantry Regiment. The ease with which the Tenth Army landings were conducted as well as the seizure of Yontan and Kadena airfields raised the obvious question as to where the

Inland and offshore Tenth Army advances. The inland movements of the Tenth Army's divisions after the 1 April landings, north and south of the Ishikawa Isthmus, are shown. Elements of the 6th Marine Division swiftly moved up the island's west coast, reaching Okinawa's most northern locale at Hedo Point on 13 April. The Motobu Peninsula was attacked by other 6th Marine Division units at the end of the first week of April resulting in the peninsula's capture by 20 April. The 1st Marine Division and the XXIV Corps' 7th and 96th Divisions moved south towards the IJA 32nd Army's main defence-line spanning the island (west-to-east) from Naha through Shuri to Yonabaru. Offshore, a Marine Reconnaissance battalion landed on Keise Shima to the west of Hagushi Bay on 26–27 March. On 12 April, elements of this battalion reconnoitred Minna Shima off the Motobu Peninsula's west coast. On 6 April, Tsugen Shima, to the south of the Katchin Peninsula, was first reconnoitred and then captured by elements of the 27th Division, which had been the floating reserve. Other elements of the 27th Division reconnoitred the Eastern Islands to the north-east of the Katchin Peninsula on 7 April. From 16–21 April, the US 77th Division attacked the island of Ie Shima, which had an airfield, located to the north-east of the Motobu Peninsula in the East China Sea. (*Meridian Mapping*)

IJA 32nd Army was. No contact was made with Ushijima's main forces as they had withdrawn to the south.

On 3 April, both Tenth Army flanking units, the 6th Marine and Army's 96th Divisions, flared out north and south, respectively. Hodge's XXIV Corps turned its drive southward as the 7th Division's 32nd Infantry Regiment moved along Nakagusuku Bay and secured the Awashi Peninsula, in conjunction with the 96th Division. Okinawa's tough combat was to now commence as XXIV Corps' units moved south down the island's narrow waist towards Shuri and Yonabaru with the 7th Division's 32nd and 184th Infantry Regiments on the eastern side and the 96th's 382nd and 383rd Infantry Regiments on the west of the line of advance.

American intelligence was unaware of the disposition and plans of the Japanese forces. Also, the concentration and number of enemy troops in the Shuri defence-line was not fully appreciated. From 4–14 April, the extent of the Japanese defences on a Naha-Shuri-Yonabaru axis was to become apparent. XXIV Corps' 96th Division, in particular, struggled with strong enemy positions from 9–12 April.

Motobu Peninsula

On 3 April, Buckner signalled Geiger's IIIAC HQ for the 6th Marine Division to seize the Motobu Peninsula and northern Okinawa. Originally, the capture of southern Okinawa was to occur before operations on the Motobu Peninsula and the island's northern half.

Riflemen from the 22nd Marines, 6th Division, mounted on tanks, hastily moved up the western coast road while other division elements marched up the island's central isthmus between Nakadomari and Ishikawa on the west and east coasts, respectively. Over the course of ten days, Shepherd's 6th Marine Division moved over 25 miles as some of his units approached the mouth of the Motobu Peninsula near Nago, which became a Marine re-supply locale along its beaches by 8 April. The 22nd Marines reached Hedo Point, the island's northern tip, by 13 April.

The 6th Marine Division's next objective was to seize the 1,500-foot elevated Yae Take, northern Okinawa's bastion in the south-west corner of the Motobu Peninsula, under the command of Colonel Takehiko Udo. This main Japanese redoubt was manned by 2,000 troops with light and medium artillery support. The Marine attack on Yae Take commenced on 14 April with Colonel Alan Shapley's 4th Marines and the attached 3rd Battalion, 29th Marines from the west while the two other 29th Marines' battalions marched on the enemy redoubt from the peninsula's centre. Marine casualties were heavy in often hand-to-hand combat. Japanese losses exceeded 1,000 killed with survivors hiding in caves. The 1st Battalion, 4th Marines gained the crest of the Yae Take on 16 April and resisted Japanese infiltration of their lines over the next two days. On 17 April, the 1st Battalion, 29th Marines captured the northern portion of the Yae Take, killing more than 700 Japanese in the process, while capturing Udo's abandoned command post. On 19 April, the 4th and 29th Marines, supported by rocket-armed Marine *Corsair* fighter-bombers, moved north to gain the northern coast of the Motobu Peninsula with resistance ending the next day. During the week-long combat to clear the Motobu Peninsula, the 6th Marine Division lost over 200 killed in action and 800 wounded and missing. Almost all of Udo's 2,000 defenders were killed in their suicidal defence.

The final sortie and sinking of the Japanese battleship *Yamato*

The 70-ton battleship *Yamato*, with its 18-inch guns and crew of 2,500, along with an escorting group of one cruiser and eight destroyers, sortied from Japan on 6 April with the intent to attack Allied shipping offshore from the Hagushi beach-head. American airstrikes of 400 carrier-borne planes were launched by TF 58 on the afternoon of 7 April. Within three hours, US Navy pilots scored hits with bombs and torpedoes and the *Yamato* capsized and exploded before reaching Okinawan waters. The cruiser and four IJN destroyers were also lost in the ill-fated Japanese surface assault.

Combat toward the Shuri defence line

By 6 April, Hodge, the XXIV Corps commander, realised that his 7th and 96th Divisions had encountered strong IJA 32nd Army positions that spanned Okinawa's width from Machinato on the west coast to Yonabaru on the east. This defence-line guarded the American approach to Naha, the island's prefectural capital on the west coast, and Shuri, in the centre, the bastion and HQ for Ushijima's 32nd Army. The IJA 62nd Division conducted delaying actions from extensive fortifications, comprising well-sited high ground, minefields and AT ditches along this line. The enemy was holed up in caves, escarpments, blockhouses and pillboxes, which were inter-connected by underground tunnels.

By 7 April, the 96th Division came to within 500 yards of Kakazu, in the vicinity of heavily defended enemy ridges. On L-Day+9, the 96th Division attacked after massive preparatory artillery (over 300 guns), naval (eighteen surface warships) and aerial (650 fighter-bomber sorties) bombardment. The 96th gained only 300 yards as the Japanese suffered over 1,500 killed in counter-attacks from 12–14 April. The XXIV Corps' Shuri offensive stalled.

By 15 April, XXIV Corps reinforcements came in the form of IIIAC and 1st Marine Division artillery, as well as the 27th Division. After four days of ground, naval and aerial bombardment of forward Japanese positions and rear troop concentration areas, Hodge scheduled his next XXIV Corps advance for 19 April with the 27th, 96th and 7th Divisions abreast of one another. However, the enemy was protected by caves and the limestone ridge complex. Unfortunately, the XXIV gains were again limited as the Japanese defenders exited their concealed positions to engage the

Americans. A 27th Division assault accompanied by thirty M4s fell short as the armour became separated from the infantry, resulting in the loss of the majority of the tanks. By the end of 19 April's combat, the 27th Division was stopped at the western end of the Urasoe-Mura escarpment. The 96th Division made limited gains along the forward slopes of Nishibaru Ridge to the east. The 7th Division on the far eastern flank of XXIV Corps attack gained no ground against tenacious Japanese defence. Continued American attacks against the Japanese entrenchments continued through 24 April without a meaningful advance. Then, on 24 April, XXIV sizable gains were made all along the Kazaku-Nishibaru Ridge line as Ushijima had withdrawn his defenders further south towards Shuri.

Geiger's IIIAC headquarters, responding to a XXIV Corps call for Marine assistance in the Shuri Line battle, dispatched the 1st Marine Division to the southern sector of Tenth Army to relieve the battered 27th Division, the latter to move north to relieve the 6th Marine Division, which was slated to head south to join the fray as part of IIIAC taking over the western zone officially on 7 May. On 27 April, the 77th Division, fresh from its seizure of Ie Shima, was to relieve the 96th Division. The 7th Division remained on Tenth Army's eastern flank.

Since 24 April, the 96th Division had been combating the IJA 32nd Army for control of the Maeda Escarpment, as it constituted a second more southerly Japanese defence ring of Shuri, on the eastern end of the Urasoe-Mura Escarpment. This height was of crucial importance as its possession provided direct vision of either the American lines or, alternatively, the Japanese Shuri defences. On 29 April, the 77th Division passed through the 96th Division lines to continue the assault on the Maeda Escarpment.

After relieving the 27th Division on 1 May, the 1st Marine Division began its attack to seize the Asa River's northern branch in an area east along the high ground between Dakeshi and Wana. The 5th Marines were to deal with Japanese positions in the difficult terrain termed the 'Awacha Pocket'. The 7th Marines were deployed farthest to the east of the division's frontage.

The XXIV Corps' 77th and 7th Divisions renewed attacks against heavily fortified enemy-held ridges, the latter unit fighting against recent Japanese reinforcements in the Kochi area. As the Japanese concentrated artillery fire against the entire American front and cloud-cover minimised US air support, only limited gains were made against Ushijima's defences at a very high cost in Marine and Army casualties. The IJA 62nd Division bore the brunt of the American assault losing over half of its complement during early May in defence of its positions and with limited counter-attacks along a line that ran from Nakoma and Uchima through the ridges north of Dakeshi to Awacha. Other Japanese units, notably the 24th Division and the 44th Independent Mixed Brigade (IMB) remained intact, though.

Japanese counter-attack, 4–5 May 1945

On the night of 2 May, the IJA 32nd Army commanders on Okinawa met, more than 100 feet below Shuri Castle, to discuss strategy. Colonel Yahara wanted a continuation of the defensive plans, which were exacting numerous American casualties. General Cho argued for a counter-offensive. Ushijima decided to unleash a major counter-attack against US XXIV Corps' front with the IJA 24th Division's 89th, 22nd and 32nd regiments along with remaining elements of his 62nd Division. The Japanese offensive was intricately planned to incorporate their limited armour, suicide boats, small amphibious landings on both costs and a wave of *kamikaze* attacks from Japan. There was also a massive preliminary enemy artillery bombardment.

The IJA 89th and 22nd Regiments attacked the US 7th Division's positions with the intent to reach Tanabaru, while the 32nd Regiment was to strike the US 77th Division south-east of Maeda to the west of Kochi. The IJA 27th Tank Regiment deployed its limited armour in support of the 32nd and 22nd Regiments. The 44th IMB assaulted to Shuri's west to protect Ushijima's left flank from the 1st Marine Division. Admiral Ota was to form four infantry battalions from his naval force to serve as an IJA 32nd Army reserve to exploit any 24th Division breakthrough. This IJA 32nd Army counter-offensive was to commence on 4–5 May.

The Japanese counter-attack failed in all sectors. Even the vehement Cho realised that the IJA 32nd Army would be defeated. The day after the counter-attack started, the 1st Marine Division captured the banks of the northern branch of the Asa River, which flowed westward along a line north of Wana through Uchima with its mouth to the north of Asa. The Marines dug-in as del Valle awaited another phase of the Japanese counter-attack that did not materialise after having incurred almost 650 casualties. During the two days of the IJA 32nd Army offensive, the army's 7th and 77th Divisions lost over 700 soldiers killed, wounded or missing. All along the XXIV Corps' lines, 6,237 Japanese bodies were counted after the battle.

Tenth Army advances to Shuri and Naha

On 5 May, Buckner renewed the Tenth Army southern drive onto the Shuri bastion. IIIAC's 6th Marine Division was the west coast's flank formation while the 1st Marine Division was situated north of the heavily defended 'Awacha Pocket'. XXIV Corps' 96th, 77th and 7th Army Divisions were abreast of each other to the east. The attack was to be along the line extending from the Asa River's mouth in the west to Yonabaru in the east.

On 9 May, elements of the 1st Division's 7th Marines attacked the mouth of the Awacha Draw with some initial gains. Japanese flanking fire, enemy infiltration and local counter-attacks slowed the advance, but del Valle's Marines continued the attack the next day. Marine tactics employed flame-thrower and demolition teams along with flame-throwing M4 tanks to overcome the Japanese Awacha defences.

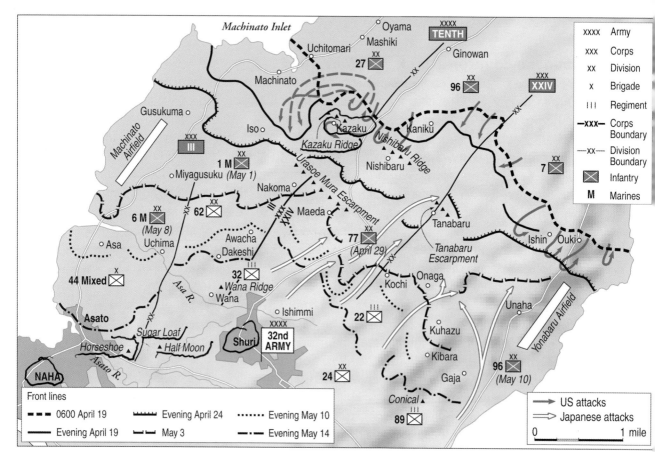

Assault on the 'Naha-Shuri' Line. Tenth Army's dates of successive advances are shown. On 19 April, XXIV Corps commenced its major attack on the outer Shuri defences with its 27th, 96th and 7th Divisions. The 27th Division's 106th Infantry Regiment, after crossing the Machinato Inlet, secured a foothold on the north-west end of the Urasoe Mura Escarpment. The 27th's 105th Infantry, with the US 193rd Tank Battalion, met fierce enemy resistance between Kakazu and Nishibaru Ridges. During the next week of combat, the Kazaku and Nishibaru Ridges and the escarpment near the village of Tanabaru were overcome, with the 96th Division held up at the Urasoe Mura Escarpment. The 7th Division's progress stalled in the vicinity of Kochi held by the IJA 22nd Regiment.

The 77th Infantry Division on 29 April relieved the 96th three days after it launched its assault on the 'Maeda Escarpment' (Hacksaw Ridge).

The 1st Marine Division reverted back to IIIAC on 7 May to continue its major southern drive with the 5th Marines requiring from 3–11 May to wrest the 'Awacha Pocket' from elements of the IJA 62nd Division. The 1st Marine Division drove onto Wana Ridge in order to reach the north-western outskirts of Shuri.

During the night of 3–4 May, the IJA 24th Division launched the major part of the IJA 32nd Army's counter-offensive in the centre and the east towards Tanabaru. From 4–6 May, XXIV Corps repulsed the Japanese assault.

On 8 May, 6th Marine Division entered the line in the south. On 10 May, the 96th Division completed its relief of the 7th Division in the south-east. Tenth Army's renewed offensive started on 11 May with (from west-to-east) the 6th Marine, 1st Marine, 77th and 96th Divisions.

After crossing the Asa River, the 6th Marine Division moved south towards the Asato River to breach the western flank of the Shuri defences by attacking the Sugar Loaf-Horseshoe-Half Moon Ridge complex from 13–19 May. Shifting away from Half Moon Ridge, the 6th Marine Division's 22nd Marines took Naha on 29 May, while units of the 1st Marine Division's 5th Marines captured Shuri Castle in the 77th Division's sector.

The IJA 32nd Army withdrew to the Kiyamu Peninsula from 25 May–4 June. (*Meridian Mapping*)

The 'Awacha Pocket' was taken on 11 May, although bypassed enemy positions now had to be reduced. Just to the south, other 7th Marines' units sustained heavy casualties along Dakeshi Ridge's 'honeycomb' of enemy pillboxes and caves on 10 May. The 7th Marines' attack continued for two more days against stubborn Japanese resistance. The Marines' capture of Dakeshi Ridge on 13 May eliminated another major Shuri defence barrier.

On 9–10 May, the 6th Marine Division moved up to the Asa River for a crossing to outflank some of the elevated terrain entrenchments to Shuri's west. During the night of 10–11 May, the Marines constructed a Bailey bridge across the Asa River, enabling armour-supported riflemen to cross the waterway. By 12 May, the 6th Marine Division, after overcoming murderous fire from overlooking rocky cliffs, reached elevated terrain above Naha and sent patrols into the locale's suburbs on the banks of the Asato.

As major parts of the Tenth Army offensive to Shuri and southwards, the US 96th Division had to confront 'Conical Hill', directly to the north-west of Yonabaru. This aptly named elevated terrain, which was really a series of ridges and other smaller hills, controlled the eastern approaches to Shuri. From 'Conical Hill', the 96th Division's soldiers were under constant observation and artillery fire by the IJA 32nd Army's eastern defences. Despite heavy fire on 11 May, the 96th Division executed some flanking manoeuvres the next day and captured some of the northern and western slopes of 'Conical Hill', thereby opening the way to Yonabaru to the east and Shuri's inner defence perimeter to the west.

Tenth Army's two corps began the attack on Shuri at 0730hrs on 14 May in an envelopment after clearing the eastern and western approaches. The major Japanese defences were west of Wana and north-east of Naha in the 1st and 6th Marine Divisions' sectors, respectively. Heavy casualties among Marine riflemen and accompanying 1st and 6th Marine Tank Battalions' armour were inflicted by Japanese artillery, AT gun- and mortar-fire as well as suicidal demolition charge rushes against the American tanks.

The 6th Division's 22nd and 29th Marines were assigned the capture of the rectangular-shaped Sugar Loaf Ridge, which constituted Ushijima's western defensive anchor to the Shuri defences. The 22nd Marines encountered strong fortified Japanese positions. Attacking Marine rifle companies incurred staggering casualty rates from an assortment of Japanese ordnance, even prior to enemy *banzai* counter-attacks from their concealed positions.

Other nearby elevated Japanese positions included Half Moon Ridge to the south-west of Sugar Loaf and Horseshoe Ridges to the south-east. All three elevated enemy positions were mutually supporting and interconnected by tunnels and galleries. The 29th Marines were ordered to take Half Moon Ridge on 15 May. Both Sugar Loaf and Half Moon Ridges remained in enemy hands after fierce combat on this day.

Continued fighting on 16 May on Sugar Loaf Ridge had so depleted the 22nd Marines' strength that General Shepherd moved this height into the 29th Marines' attack sector, which had been heavily engaged at Half Moon Ridge. A three-battalion tank-infantry assault on 17 May by the 29th Marines on Sugar Loaf failed, despite an immense preparatory artillery barrage with field artillery and naval gunfire. On 18 May, the 29th Marines made progress against both Sugar Loaf and Half Moon Ridges, but enemy fire from their nearby positions atop Horseshoe Ridge prevented seizure by the Americans. Since Tenth Army first began its offensive against the Shuri defences on 11 May, the 6th Division's 22nd and 29th Marines suffered almost 4,000 total casualties.

From 8 April into mid-May, the American offensive gained an average of only 130 yards per day while incurring thousands of casualties. To Ushijima, the 6th Marine Division's advance towards the Asato River threatened a breakthrough at Naha. To block the Marine drive, Ushijima moved four naval battalions to strengthen his IJA 44th IMB. Geiger's IIIAC headquarters released the 4th Marines from corps reserve to replace the 29th Marines, who went into 6th Marine Division reserve on 19 May. Just prior to the scheduled relief of the 29th Marines, a strong Japanese counter-attack hit the Americans' open right flank just below the lip of Horseshoe Ridge. The 29th Marines had to withdraw to the northern slop of Sugar Loaf Ridge prior to their relief.

At 0800hrs on 20 May, two assault battalions of the 4th Marines, supported by the Marines' 6th Tank Battalion and 5th Rocket Detachment, along with XXIV Corps' 91st Chemical Company with their 4.2-inch mortars, attacked both Half Moon and Horseshoe Ridges. The Marines made early substantial gains of about 200 yards. However, determined enemy resistance from entrenched Japanese infantry on the two ridges halted the 4th Marines' advance. By the day's end, the customary massive Japanese counter-attack was heralded by increased bursts of enemy white phosphorus shells and coloured smoke. Almost 700 Japanese attacked the positions of Companies K and L, 3rd Battalion, 4th Marines. US Navy gunfire support-ships and six artillery battalions' prepared concentrations aided the Marines along with the timely commitment of 3rd Battalion's Company B to blunt the Japanese counter-attack. By the next morning, more than 500 Japanese dead were counted.

Wana Draw and attack on Shuri's north-western defences

The 1st Marine Division and the Army's 77th Division were to overcome the Wana defences to the north-west of Shuri. The 1st Marine Division, after they had just cleared heavily fortified Dakeshi in their southern advance, were to attack the Wana Draw, with the southern branch of the Asa River running through it and the northern part of Shuri. The Wana Draw was an attacker's nightmare as it combined prepared enemy-fortified positions and the 'force multiplier' of difficult terrain. Japanese fire from various ordnance rained shells down on the del Valle's Marines from the reverse slope of Wana Ridge and Hill 55 at the southern tip of the ridge. The 5th Marines commander, Colonel John H. Griebel, noted that the Wana Draw was 'another gorge like the one at Awacha ... and would have to be thoroughly pounded before it could be taken'. Armour and airstrikes were unleashed on 16 May with a tremendous expenditure of shells, bombs and napalm. On 17 May, platoon-sized elements of the 7th Marines were able to seize positions atop Hill 55 and maintained their gains the next day after being re-supplied by tanks that brought in rations and ammunition. On 19 May, the 5th Marines were prepared to assault the mouth of the Wana Draw. The next day, this unit gained territory that ran from Hill 55 south-west to the Naha-Shuri Road, which skirted the northern tip of Shuri. Then, torrential rains commenced on 21–22 May as the 5th Marines continued their assault on Wana Ridge and 110 Meter Hill, and were to continue for the remainder of the month.

On 15 May, the 77th Division moved on Shuri itself and its assault sector over-lapped in some areas with the 1st Marine Division at sites such as 110 Meter Hill, on the north-western outskirts of the Japanese bastion defended by the IJA 89th Regiment. On 17 May, elements of the 77th Division captured some commanding terrain, which included 'Chocolate Drop', in close proximity to Shuri and Ishimmi. On 19 May, the 77th Division continued to reduce Japanese positions on 110 Meter Hill, Ishimmi Ridge, and along the reverse slopes of 'Flat Top' and 'Dick' Ridges. By 21 May, 77th Division troops entered the outskirts of Shuri.

On the right flank of the Tenth Army, 96th Division troops attacked a series of ridges ('Oboe', 'Love', 'Conical', 'Hogback', 'Sugar') on the eastern end of Okinawa between Shuri and Yonabaru, defended by the IJA 22nd Regiment. With the continuation of the heavy rain for over a week, which created a morass of mud for movement and limited air cover, Tenth Army advances were reduced to probing patrols as the major offensive effort ground to a halt. Outposts of the 96th Division, situated south and west of 'Conical Hill', were isolated from rear echelon support and contended with frequent Japanese infiltrations and local enemy counter-attacks.

To eventually support the efforts of the 77th, Hodge had ordered the 7th Division the previous day to assemble to the north of 'Conical Hill'. By 25 May, the 7th Division had made gains into the south-eastern end of the Shuri defences. In order to maintain his Shuri front, Ushijima consolidated two flank defence-lines. An eastern one started on the south-west slopes of 'Conical Hill' and extended to the west of Yonawa to the village of Chan, further to the south-west. A more western Japanese defence-line began at the southern end of Shuri and moved southwards.

The next day, 26 May, Marine observers noted that a large number of Japanese troops and vehicles were departing Shuri for the south. The Japanese were moving the remnants of their 24th and 62nd Divisions along with the 44th IMB towards a line at Yaeju Dake-Yazu Dake Escarpment. In all, Ushijima evacuated approximately

11,000 infantry and 22,000 other troops. American naval gunfire, Marine fighter bombers, field artillery and tank gunfire rained down on the retreating Japanese resulting in hundreds of enemy killed and vehicles destroyed. Although Buckner ordered a full-scale attack all along the front to prevent Ushijima from establishing new, secure defence-lines, torrential rain and poor terrain limited Tenth Army interdiction efforts.

The Japanese defence of Shuri began to cease on 28 May when 1st Division Marines and 77th Division soldiers seized the city's high ground to the north and east. Shuri Castle was captured by the 1st Battalion, 5th Marines, 1st Division on 29 May. Ushijima's rear-guard at Shuri had enabled the IJA 32nd Army commander to extract his surviving forces to the south rather than being caught in a double envelopment envisioned by Buckner.

The 6th Marine Division at Naha

On 21 May, the 4th and 22nd Marines, 6th Division advanced towards the north-east outskirts of Naha halfway between Horseshoe Ridge and the Asato River. To facilitate this movement Companies K and L, 3rd Battalion, 4th Marines had to destroy deadly Japanese mortar positions emplaced amid the interior of Horseshoe Ridge. Also, on 21 May, a 6th Marine Division's tank-infantry advance on Half Moon Ridge to the east was slowed by intense enfilading mortar-fire from the heights of Shuri to the east. Shepherd shifted his division's efforts onto Naha and the North Fork of the Kokuba River as the devastating Japanese shelling precluded the 6th Marine Division's eastward envelopment of Shuri.

Early on 23 May, Marine patrols moved 400 yards south of the Asato River under moderate fire. Then, two battalions crossed the river in force under a smokescreen. During the overnight of 23–24 May, the 6th Engineer Battalion, under the command of Major Paul F. Sackett, built a Bailey bridge suitable for tank crossing. Under darkness on 24 May, two squads from Major Anthony Walker's 6th Marine Division's Scout and Sniper Reconnaissance Company crossed the lower Asato River and met no resistance in the streets of north-western Naha. The remainder of the Reconnaissance Company then crossed the river on 25 May and penetrated deep into Naha's deserted rubble interior west of the north-south-running canal that divides the locale in half.

On the morning of 27 May, Company G of the 2nd Battalion, 22nd Marines crossed the Asato River and passed through the Reconnaissance Company's lines into the western portion of the city against only minimal Japanese resistance. The remainder of the 2nd Battalion, 22nd Marines advanced and captured the elevated terrain just to the north of the Kokuba Estuary. Naha was located at the mouth of the Kokuba River that was dominated by the high ground of the Oroku Peninsula across the channel to the south. The capital city's utility served as a route southwards. As the

22nd Marines moved unopposed south through Naha towards the Kokuba Estuary, a platoon scouted the approaches to Ona-Yama Island situated in the Kokuba Channel at the southern end of the Naha Canal on 28 May. After receiving heavy Japanese automatic weapons fire, the Marine patrol retreated. Nonetheless, all of Naha to the canal's west and north of Kokuba Estuary was controlled by Shepherd's Marines.

On 28 May, the Marine 6th Engineer Battalion reconnoitred all bridge crossings across the Naha Canal and installed a Jeep and two foot-bridges over it during the pre-dawn hours of 29 May. The engineers worked in rain and darkness, having man-handled the bridging materials to the various sites, all while under enemy fire. By 0430hrs, elements of the 1st Battalion, 22nd Marines were across the canal and organised on its eastern shore in the vicinity of Telegraph Hill in east Naha, where combat continued throughout the day without much in the way of gains. On 30 May, the 2nd and 3rd Battalions, 22nd Marines moved across the canal and through the 1st Battalion's positions. These 6th Marine Division's battalions fought until darkness across open ground without much cover against stiffening Japanese resistance notably from enemy automatic weapons emplaced in burial tombs on Hill 27, which was eventually seized by a Marine tank-infantry assault.

The Kokuba Hills extended eastward from Naha's south-eastern edge along the north side of the Kokuba Estuary and its Japanese defensive emplacements guarded the southern route to the rear of the Shuri defences. It was vital for the enemy to interdict a Marine envelopment of the Shuri bastion from Naha. Japanese defensive operations, under IJA 44th IMB HQ control, were previously re-located from Shuri to the Kokuba Hills on 22–23 May. The Japanese, after western Naha's evacuation, took up the defence of these hills and the eastern section of the city.

Since crossing the upper Asato River on 23 May, the 4th Marines painstakingly moved forward through this flooded terrain. On 28 May, the 4th Marines were to advance onto eastern Naha, following a nine-battalion preparatory artillery bombard-ment of suspected Japanese positions left in the capital city, just before their relief by the 29th Marines. The 4th Marines had incurred more than 1,100 casualties since it had relieved the 29th Marines earlier in the month during the intense fighting for the Sugar Loaf-Horseshoe-Half Moon Ridge masses north-east of Naha.

After the Marine capture of Hill 27 on 30 May, the eastward-advancing 22nd and 29th Marines ran into Japanese defences on Hill 46 north of the Kokuba Estuary. Another Marine tank-infantry assault moved against the hill with the support of American artillery. On 1 June, the 22nd and 29th Marines broke through the Japanese defences and seized Hill 98 along with the northern fork of the Kokuba River, which was to be crossed on 2 June unopposed as the enemy withdrew the night before.

Shepherd next planned to seize the Oroku Peninsula, on which Naha Airfield was situated, with both a ground and amphibious assault. The 6th Marine Division's Scout and Sniper Reconnaissance Company crossed Naha Harbour in rubber boats and infiltrated the northern portion of the peninsula on the night of 1–2 June. Although receiving enemy fire, Walker's scouts were able to glean that the Oroku Peninsula's northern beaches were lightly defended and, thereby, suitable for LVTs to land. IIIAC HQ ordered Shepherd late on the morning of 2 June to the probability of reorienting his 6th Marine Division towards the Oroku Peninsula. Geiger then directed the 1st Marine Division to assume responsibility of the 6th Marine Division's zone, excluding Naha, as of 2 June.

Battle of the Oroku Peninsula, 4–6 June

During the pre-dawn hours of 4 June, Shepherd landed his rested 1st and 2nd Battalions, 4th Marines in seventy-two LVTs, under naval gunfire, along the Nishikoku Beaches on the Oroku Peninsula's north-east coast. They were followed by the 29th Marines in the previously used LVTs that had returned to the mainland, along with LCMs and LCTs bringing in tanks and the 4th Marines Special Weapons Company to support the attacking infantry. The assaulting 6th Marine Division units were to then move southwards towards the central high ground. Also, Ona Yama Island, located in the channel separating Naha from the Oroku Peninsula, was to be captured as a forward 6th Marine Division logistics and support base.

The initial Marines who went ashore at 0600hrs faced only scattered Japanese machine-gunfire 300 yards inland from the beaches. Within an hour, the armour of Company A, 6th Tank Battalion as well as self-propelled 105mm HMC landed to support the 2nd Battalion, 4th Marines. Another company of tanks from the 6th Tank Battalion landed soon after to support the 1st Battalion, 4th Marines. Eventually, inland minefields and increasing enemy resistance slowed the tank-infantry advance. The 3rd Battalion, 4th Marines landed at 0900hrs and was tasked with the seizure of Naha Airfield, the most highly developed aerodrome on Okinawa. An hour later, Shepherd ordered two battalions of the 29th Marines, now under Colonel William J. Whaling, to move onto the peninsula to the left of the 4th Marines. By nightfall of 4 June, the 6th Division's invasion was 1,500 yards inland but enemy resistance, rain and minefields began to slow the advance.

The Oroku assault continued on 5 June, but the 4th Marines were halted by an enemy strongpoint near Toma. Enemy artillery stopped Marine armour. However, the 15th Marines used counter-battery fire against Japanese gun-flashes, silencing four 120mm dual-purpose, one 6-inch and several smaller calibre field guns. Muddy fields also limited Marine armour support so 37mm AT guns were used to reduce Japanese fortified cave positions with direct gunfire at near-point-blank range. In all, the 4th Marines gained 1,000 yards on 5 June.

On 5 June, the 29th Marines advance was slowed down near elevated terrain (Hill 57) at the outskirts of Oroku Mura in the centre of the peninsula. Shepherd's plan was to compress the Japanese onto the high ground near Tomigusuki. Eventually, the Japanese naval force was confined to an area of approximately 1 mile.

The two 6th Marine Division assault regiments encountered strong well-camouflaged enemy defences amid hilly terrain running north-west to south-east along the length of the Oroku Peninsula. The Japanese defenders were from Admiral Ota's Naval Force and were underestimated to be of approximately 2,000 men. Their training and organisation was below the standards of the IJA 32nd Army. Although their personal weaponry was deficient, the naval troops had stripped machine-guns as well as 20mm and 40mm cannons from aircraft and had placed them in camouflaged positions overlooking minefields and other routes to the defended hills. Reducing enemy positions was painstakingly slow and continued through 10 June, when the Japanese launched local counter-attacks resulting in 200 enemy naval troops killed. During the ten days of fighting on the Oroku Peninsula, 5,000 Japanese were killed.

Shepherd unleashed eight battalions of infantry with armour support against the remaining Japanese defenders on the morning of 11 June. The Marines gradually overcame Japanese positions atop Hills 62 and 53, resulting in a dissolution of the naval force the next day. On 12 June, 159 Japanese surrendered, the first substantial group of prisoners. Others chose suicide by a variety of methods, including Admiral Ota, who was found with his dead staff members as well as 200 other bodies at an elaborate warren of underground headquarters. To attest to the ferocity and tenacity with which the Japanese naval personnel fought on the Oroku Peninsula, the 6th Marine Division lost 1,600 men killed or wounded, which was proportionately greater than the casualty list at the Shuri defences, where the 1st Marine and 77th Division faced the IJA 32nd Army.

Assaulting the last Japanese defence lines

As early as 22 May, Ushijima and his staff decided that a prolonged defence of Shuri was futile. The IJA 32nd Army commanders decided against a defence of the Chinen Peninsula. However, they established a line of fortified natural positions on the Kiyamu Peninsula on Okinawa's southern tip. The Kiyamu Peninsula's defence-line was dominated by the Yaeju Dake-Yuza Dake Escarpment, replete with caves for defences and protection as well as provisions and ammunition. To execute his withdrawal from Shuri, Ushijima's rear-guard was to hold their positions against the 1st Marine and 77th Divisions until 31 May. The IJA 24th Division and the remnants of the 62nd Division, the latter having borne the brunt of the Shuri defence, along with the remainder of the 89th Regiment and 44th IMB, were to make their stand at Okinawa's southern end. The American invading force had killed an estimated 63,000 Japanese troops while capturing fewer than 500. At this point of the campaign, the US Tenth Army had incurred more than 5,300 deaths and almost 24,000 wounded.

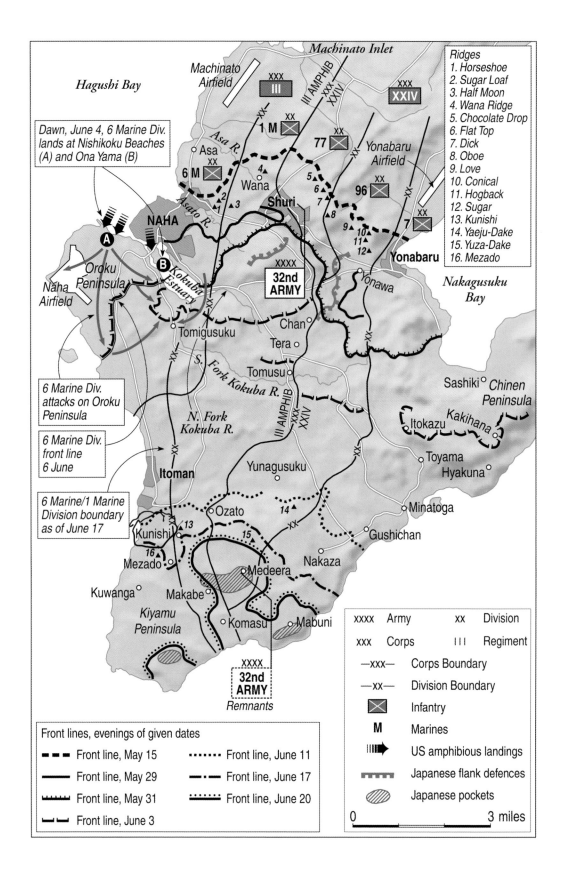

Hagushi Bay

Machinato Inlet

Machinato Airfield

Ridges
1. Horseshoe
2. Sugar Loaf
3. Half Moon
4. Wana Ridge
5. Chocolate Drop
6. Flat Top
7. Dick
8. Oboe
9. Love
10. Conical
11. Hogback
12. Sugar
13. Kunishi
14. Yaeju-Dake
15. Yuza-Dake
16. Mezado

III

III AMPHIB

XXIV

XXIV

1 M

77

Asa R.

Asa

6 M

Wana

4

5

6

7

Yonabaru Airfield

96

Shuri

2

3

1

8

9

7

Asato R.

10

11

12

Dawn, June 4, 6 Marine Div. lands at Nishikoku Beaches (A) and Ona Yama (B)

A

NAHA

B

Kokuba Estuary

32nd ARMY

Yonawa

Yonabaru

Nakagusuku Bay

Oroku Peninsula

Naha Airfield

Tomigusuku

Chan

Tera

Tomusu

6 Marine Div. attacks on Oroku Peninsula

S. Fork Kokuba R.

N. Fork Kokuba R.

Sashiki

Chinen Peninsula

Itokazu

Kakihana

6 Marine Div. front line 6 June

III AMPHIB

XXIV

Yunagusuku

Toyama

Hyakuna

Itoman

Minatoga

6 Marine/1 Marine Division boundary as of June 17

Ozato

14

Gushichan

Kunishi

13

15

Nakaza

16

Mezado

Medeera

Kuwanga

Makabe

Kiyamu Peninsula

Komasu

Mabuni

32nd ARMY
Remnants

| xxxx | Army | xx | Division |
| xxx | Corps | III | Regiment |

—xxx— Corps Boundary

—xx— Division Boundary

Infantry

M Marines

US amphibious landings

Japanese flank defences

Japanese pockets

0   3 miles

Front lines, evenings of given dates

- - - Front line, May 15   ····· Front line, June 11

——— Front line, May 29   —·—· Front line, June 17

—⊥⊥⊥— Front line, May 31   ····· Front line, June 20

— — Front line, June 3

From nature's standpoint, a vigorous pursuit of the retreating Japanese was precluded by storms, poor visibility and mud.

On 3 June, the US 7th Division had reached Okinawa's east coast, cutting off the Chinen Peninsula. The 7th Division's three regiments were now near Itokazu and Toyama to move south-west onto the Kiyamu Peninsula. To the west, the US 96th Division also advanced against minimal resistance as it seized Tera on 3 June. To the west of XXIV Corps, the 1st Marine Division advanced against only Japanese battalion-sized opposition. Torrential rains, which turned the XXIV Corps' 6,000 yards of frontage into soft clay, limited American supply to airdrops. However, by 5–6 June, the downpours curtailed.

On 7 June, the 1st Marine Division broke through to Itoman, north-west of Kunishi Ridge, the latter being the western end of the enemy's Kiyamu Peninsula's defence-line. Four days later, the 1st Division's 7th Marines encountered stiffening Japanese resistance at Kunishi Ridge, a mile-long coral escarpment replete with enemy-occupied caves. To get there, the Marines had to traverse under enemy fire 'No Man's Valley', an 800-yard broad expanse of grasslands and rice paddies. The 7th Marines' commander, Colonel Edward Snedeker, ordered a night attack with two of his battalions for early on 12 June. The 7th Marines' assault battalions reached Kunishi Ridge's crest completely surprising the defenders. However, the Japanese recovered and rained fire from their caves on the forward and reverse slopes on advancing Marine units in the open at dawn. The Marines atop the crest of the ridge were isolated and needed to be re-supplied by air-drops and reinforced by Marine M4 tanks carrying in infantrymen. The 7th Marines held on to the crest despite continuous Japanese efforts to dislodge them.

US Tenth Army attack on IJA 32nd Army's final redoubts. After the IJA 32nd Army withdrew to the south of Shuri with flanking defences situated between Shuri and Yonawa, Admiral Ota's 10,000-strong Naval Base Force, on 28 May, elected to return the Oroku Peninsula. Elements of the 6th Marine Division's 4th and 29th Marines landed against Japanese opposition along the Nishikoku beaches on the north coast of the peninsula and seized Ona Yama in the Naha Channel on 4 June. On the eastern coast, the 7th Division moved onto the Chinen Peninsula. The 1st Marine and 96th Divisions continued their drive south of Shuri in the centre of the island.

By 11 June, the remnants of the IJA 32nd Army held a line running from the south of Itoman through the Kunishi Ridge in the west to the Yaeju-Dake and Yuza-Dake Ridge masses in the island's centre.

On 15 June, the 2nd Marine Division's 8th Marines was attached to the 1st Marine Division. On 17 June, elements of the 7th Division overran a 44th IMB enemy pocket to the south-west of Nakaza. Five days later, this US Army division surrounded the IJA 32nd Army's HQ south of Mabuni. On 20–22 June, 96th Division combated an enemy pocket comprising the IJA 24th Division between Makabe and Medeera. The 1st Marine Division eliminated an enemy pocket comprising the remnants of the IJA 62nd Division inland from the island's southern tip. Okinawa was declared secure, except for the ensuing days' mopping-up operations, during the evening hours of 21 June. (*Meridian Mapping*)

At 0330hrs on 14 June, the 1st Marines assaulted Kunishi Ridge after a preparatory artillery bombardment of thirty minutes. Slow progress was made and the attack was supported by elements of the 5th Marines. By the end of 16 June, Kunishi Ridge was captured and the 1st Marine Division moved onto the Mezado Ridge mass.

On 17 June, fresh from their hard-fought victory on the Oroku Peninsula, the 6th Marine Division passed through the 1st Division's 7th Marines to aid in the assault on Mezado Ridge. In the ensuing combat among the hills of this terrain mass, the IJA 22nd Regiment was almost completely wiped out. Geiger committed further reinforcements to his IIIAC advance in the form of the 8th Marines, 2nd Marine Division.

The 8th Marines were sent to Saipan shortly after L-Day. On 3 June, two 8th Marines battalions landed unopposed at Iheya Shima, 15 miles north-west of Okinawa's northern tip. On 9 June, Aguni Shima, 30 miles west of Okinawa, was assaulted by an 8th Marines battalion and, again, no resistance was met. These offshore islands were to be developed into long-range radar and fighter-director facilities by the US Navy after their substantial losses at the hands of Japanese *kamikaze* attacks. After these unopposed 8th Marine assaults, these battalions were then added as fresh units for the last push onto the IJA 32nd Army defences in the Kiyamu Peninsula.

On 18 June, the 8th Marines, 2nd Division drove on the Mezado Ridge to relieve the 7th Marines, 1st Division. Buckner wanted to see the 8th Marines in action despite being warned of nearby enemy flanking fire. Buckner was atop a coral ridge at a 3rd Battalion, 8th Marines' OP, when a Japanese 47mm AT shell struck the boulders that the Tenth Army commander was situated in. Either a shell or rock fragment hit Buckner in the chest, mortally wounding him. On 19 June, Geiger was promoted to the rank of lieutenant-general and officially appointed Commanding General, Tenth Army. US Army Lieutenant-General Joseph W. Stilwell landed on Okinawa on 23 June and relieved Geiger of the Tenth Army command.

As the 1st Marine Division (and attached 8th Marines) continued its southern drive, Hodge's XXIV Corps, comprising the 7th and 96th Divisions, to the east attacked the Yuza Dake-Yaeju Dake Escarpment on 9 June. This terrain barrier was a collection of hill masses that spanned the entire XXIV Corps front. At 290 feet, the Yaeju-Dake peak was the highest point in this 4-mile-long cliff. The Army soldiers had dubbed the Yaeju-Dake peak the 'Big Apple'. The Yuza-Dake was situated at the western end of XXIV line and then tapered off into the Kunishi Ridge to the west, the latter in the 1st Marine Division's sector. These hill masses also extended east through Gushichan to Hill 95, the eastern anchor. East of Hill 95 on the island's Pacific coast was a 300-foot drop to the waters below. The only area through this formidable terrain obstacle was in the 7th Division's sector via a narrow valley south through Nakaza, which was under enemy observation and gunfire.

Earlier, on 3–4 June, Ushijima's 11,000 retreating infantry forces from Shuri reached the Yaeju-Dake and Yazu-Dake peaks before the Americans and had holed up in caves and crevices within and behind the escarpment wall. Two weeks of bloody combat were required for these US Army divisions to reduce Japanese resistance along this elevated terrain. In the Japanese defensive centre, Ushijima positioned the IJA 24th Division's 89th Infantry Regiment near Yuza Dake and extending to the west to the town of Itoman on the coast north of the Kunishi Ridge. The Yaeju Dake peak and the eastern flank were held by the 44th IMB (2nd and 15th Independent Mixed Regiments) to contest the US 7th Division advance. The remnants of the IJA 62nd Division were placed in reserve near Makabe.

On 6 June, the 381st Infantry Regiment, 96th Division probed Yaeju-Dake peak and was driven back by heavily entrenched enemy gunfire positions from within caves. Over the next three days, the 96th Division blasted the coral escarpment. On 10 June, both the 381st and 383rd Infantry Regiments fired on the peaks of Yaeju-Dake and Yuza-Dake, respectively, with the latter formation also attacking the town of Yuza the next day. The 383rd's battle for Yuza was a three-day 'see-saw' one with the Japanese driven out during daytime combat, only to re-occupy the town each night. Also, on 11 June the 381st Infantry Regiment with heavy tank and artillery support moved on the caves of 60-foot-high 'Big Apple Peak', which the enemy still controlled by the end of 12 June. By 15–16 June, the 383rd, exhausted by thirty-five days of continuous combat, went into reserve as the 382nd Infantry Regiment proceeded against Yuza-Dake peak.

From 6–9 June, the elements of the 7th Division's 184th Infantry Regiment faced tenacious enemy resistance on an 800-yard coral ridge proximate to Hill 95. The 7th Division's 32nd Infantry Regiment received the arduous task of reducing Hill 95's caves and the coral ridge to its front in order for the far eastern wing of XXIV Corps to secure a lodgement on the southern lower end of the Yaeju-Dake peak. Although elements of the 32nd Infantry Regiment had consolidated their position along Yaeju-Dake's south-eastern tip by 9 June, it was not until 11 June when a battalion from each of the 184th and 32nd Regiments reached the high end of Hill 95. American infantry, artillery and tanks reducing one enemy cave position after another with the widespread use of flame-throwing weapons proved decisive.

In the pre-dawn hours of 12 June, the 7th Division's 17th Infantry Regiment made a night attack, without artillery preparation to preserve stealth, on Yaeju-Dake peak. Within four hours of starting their attack, with the benefit of a heavy fog to obscure their movements, companies from the 1st Battalion, 17th Infantry Regiment seized their objective on the Yaeju-Dake peak. Over a hundred enemy soldiers were killed.

Throughout 17 June, the XXIV Corps resisted Japanese counter-attacks as the defending enemy infantry units were also becoming depleted. Ushijima's HQ was one of the last Japanese bastions to be defended. Ushijima sent his last message to his troops on 19 June. Three days later, at noon on 22 June, Ushijima and Cho committed ritual suicide by *hara-kiri*. Sporadic fighting continued along all aspects of the American advance, with a dwindling number of enemy pockets on 20 June. On 21 June, organised resistance ended in the 6th Marine Division zone on the island's west coast. Elsewhere, ever-increasing numbers of soldiers and civilians emerged from caves and surrendered. However, in some sectors of the XXIV Corps front, Japanese soldiers fought to the last man.

6th Division Marines pull an ammunition cart through the Okinawan village of Nakaoshi in April. A divisional Marine Reconnaissance Company had scouted Nago at the south-eastern tip of the Motobu Peninsula and then crossed the peninsula's base towards Nakaoshi, which was struck by a surprise Japanese attack on 17 April that drove through a 6th Engineer Battalion command post, water point, and supply installation. (*NARA*)

Soldiers from the 96th Division move behind an M4 medium tank of the 763rd Tank Battalion that was applying gunfire onto Japanese entrenched positions in front of the unit's methodical advance. The 96th Division fought against one of the strongest enemy positions, a series of ridges named 'Love', 'Conical', 'Oboe', 'Sugar', that spanned from Shuri towards Nakagusuku Bay during mid-May. Tank-infantry cooperation was paramount to reducing these Japanese fortified locales. *(NARA)*

Soldiers from the 184th Infantry Regiment, 7th Division, manhandle artillery shells up some rough, jagged terrain along the eastern end of the XXIV Corps southern advance against a new Japanese defence-line along the Yaeju-Dake and Yazu-Dake peaks in early June. *(NARA)*

(**Opposite, above**) Part of a 6th Marine Division's Special Weapons Company with their 37mm AT gun in late May covering the approach to a Kokuba Estuary bridge. After Shepherd's Marines captured parts of Naha and the Kokuba Estuary, steps were immediately taken to defend these areas. Eight 37mm AT guns were situated along the northern bank of the Kokuba Estuary behind the sea-wall there. (*NARA*)

(**Opposite, below**) Soldiers from the US Army's 381st Infantry Regiment, 96th Division move cautiously in a probing effort of the Yaeju-Dake peak ('Big Apple Ridge') on 11 June. After a slight penetration of the enemy's new defence-line, the Americans were driven back by a heavy enemy gunfire. (*NARA*)

(**Above**) Riflemen from a 6th Marine Division's tank-mounted Reconnaissance Company move up the western coast road towards Chuta to ascertain the Japanese strength on the Motobu Peninsula in early April. Stiffening Japanese resistance indicated that the enemy was located there in some force. Colonel Victor F. Bleasdale's 29th Marines' began their advance on the main enemy force on the peninsula on 9 April. (*USMC*)

An American flag is raised by a company of soldiers under the command of Major William Carness from the 2nd Battalion, 306th Infantry Regiment, 77th Division atop the 500-foot-high Iegusugu Pinnacle to break a deadlock on the island of Ie Shima. From 16–21 April, the 77th Division combated the Japanese on this island to the west of the Motobu Peninsula to both seize an airfield as well as silence enemy enfilading fire on the 6th Marine Division. During the struggle for the 'Pinnacle' from 19–21 April, the 77th Division's assistant commander, Brigadier-General Edwin H. Randle, described it as 'a damned highly fortified position with caves three stories deep, each concrete with machine-guns in and under'. (USAMHI)

Soldiers from the 96th Division march along a winding road towards one of the fortified enemy ridges to the east of the Japanese 32nd Army's bastion at Shuri on 21 May. By the end of May, the Americans were exhausted with the 96th Division having been in the line for fifty out of sixty-one days. (*NARA*)

(**Opposite, above**) Marines watch from a safe distance the detonation of a demolition charge to destroy a Japanese fortified position along an enemy ridgeline. Both Marine demolition and flame-thrower teams 'blasted and burned' into enemy gun and mortar positions in caves, tombs and crevices in their trek onto Shuri and further south. (*NARA*)

(**Opposite, below**) Soldiers from the 17th Infantry Regiment, 7th Division make limited progress on the eastern end of the XXIV Corps' attack from 6–9 June. In company strength, the soldiers were able to advance up to a mile through green knolls at the base of Yaeju-Dake Escarpment's rocky, jagged terrain. (*Author's Collection*)

(**Above**) Marine riflemen with their weapons trained on the opening of an enemy-held ridge's cave just after a demolition charge was detonated. 'Blowtorch and corkscrew' tactics with flame-throwers or flame-throwing armour along with demolition teams, respectively, were required as even Allied 16-inch calibre shells from offshore warships failed to penetrate deep underground Japanese installations. With such a tactical approach, enemy positions were painstakingly reduced one at a time. A Japanese 47mm AT gun battalion commander commented after being captured that this combined arms American tactic could penetrate any enemy 'defence-line, however well protected'. (*NARA*)

(**Opposite, above**) XXIV Corps soldiers advance across an open plain as they move on enemy-defended ridges (*background*). During the Shuri offensive in May, both the 77th and 96th Divisions contested these Japanese-fortified heights, one being the Maeda Escarpment. The 77th Division's 307th Infantry Regiment took over the Maeda Escarpment part of the line from the 96th Division's 381st Infantry Regiment on 29 April, the latter formation suffering over 500 casualties over four days of combat against elements of the IJA 24th Division. On 5 May, the 307th Infantry Regiment captured the east end of the escarpment after using demolitions to clean out a 'maze of caves, tunnels, and pillboxes'. An after-action report noted that when an American tank fired some phosphorus shells into one cave, within minutes smoke emanated from over thirty other hidden openings on the slope. This locale received the moniker Hacksaw Ridge. (*NARA*)

(**Opposite, below**) A Marine with his Thompson 0.45-inch calibre SMG runs across open terrain atop Sugar Loaf Ridge. The first encounter of the 22nd Marines, 6th Division with the Japanese guarding Sugar Loaf Ridge occurred on 12 May was inadvertent. Sugar Loaf and the surrounding ridges, Horseshoe and Half Moon, were situated in a triangular position, to afford the Japanese defenders on any of the three ridges a tactical advantage to bring mutually supporting, enfilading machine-gun and mortar-fire onto the approaching Marines. This was in addition to the Japanese commanding excellent fields of fire to the north-west from Shuri Heights. The enemy's use of artillery from this elevated terrain hampered the 6th Marine Division's advance from the Asa River in the north to the Asato River to the south of these ridges. The fighting on Sugar Loaf Ridge continued until its capture on 18–19 May. (*NARA*)

(**Above**) Five 6th Division Marines atop Sugar Loaf Ridge. On 18 May, a co-ordinated attack by Company D, 29th Marines captured this height. Marine artillery had bombarded the forward slopes of the ridge while tanks fired into a maze of Japanese caves on the reverse slopes. The enemy resisted with suicidal demolition rushes against the armour as well as field pieces firing on Marine rocket trucks to support the infantry assault. On 19 May, the 4th Marines relieved the exhausted 29th Marines. The 4th Marines were still to engage the enemy on Horseshoe and Half Moon Ridges on 20–21 May and then shift their attack west to Naha, the island's capital city. (*NARA*)

(**Opposite, above**) A four-man Marine stretcher detail doing the grim work of bringing one of their dead comrades down from Sugar Loaf Ridge. In ten days of combat for Sugar Loaf Ridge, there were over 2,600 Marines killed or wounded, including three battalion and eleven company commanders. (*NARA*)

(**Above**) On 10 May, L Company, the 3rd Battalion, 5th Marines, 1st Division advances into an open, 75-yard area called 'Death Valley'. This rough terrain was essentially a draw between two hills in the vicinity of the 'Awacha Pocket', north-east of Dakeshi and south of Awacha. During an eight-hour period, the Marines suffered 125 casualties crossing this particular draw in combat with elements of the IJA 62nd Division. After 'Death Valley' and the 'Awacha Pocket', the 1st Marine Division was to become heavily engaged in the battle for Wana Ridge just to the north of the Asa River to Shuri's west. (*NARA*)

(**Opposite, below**) A 6th Marine Division 0.30-inch calibre Browning M1917, water-cooled MMG in its position providing indirect cover fire on the outskirts of Naha. Shepherd's division had captured 'Sugar Loaf' and Horseshoe Ridges, on 21 May. However, after five gruelling days of combat, the 6th Marine Division cancelled its attack on Half Moon Ridge's reverse slopes and halted its eastward envelopment of Shuri. Shepherd decided to move on Naha and the Kokuba River. On 23–24 May, the 6th Marine Division began to cross the Asato River under moderate enemy fire via Bailey bridges and a tank crossing. On 25 May, squads of the division's Reconnaissance Company crossed the lower Asato River and met no enemy resistance as they entered the north-western aspects of Naha. (*NARA*)

(**Opposite, above**) A squad of 6th Division Marines races into a building in the northern part of Naha. On 27 May, a company from the 22nd Marines 2nd Battalion moved on to the western part of Naha after crossing the Asato River and passing through the lines held by the division's Reconnaissance Company, who had entered the capital city previously. The 22nd Marines then worked their way through, clearing the demolished buildings. (*NARA*)

(**Above**) Two 6th Division Marines from the 2nd Battalion, 22nd Marines take cover behind the ruins of a house and return fire from snipers across the Naha Channel. Naha is located in a wide coastal flat at the Kokuba Estuary. The capital city was dominated by the Oroku Peninsula's high ground across the Naha Channel to the south and by a ridge that ran north-east to south-west along the estuary. In the middle of the Naha Channel was the island of Ona Yama. Marines reconnoitring the approaches to Ona Yama Island received sniper- and machine-gunfire. (*NARA*)

(**Opposite, below**) A soldier from the 305th Infantry Regiment, 77th Division fires his M1 Garand semi-automatic rifle at the mouth of a Japanese cave at the base of the Yuza-Dake Escarpment on 17 June. This east-west running hill mass was defended by elements of the IJA 89th Regiment, 24th Division. The infantryman to the left uses his hand-held Set Complete Radio or Signal Corps Radio (SCR)-536, commonly called a 'walkie-talkie', to assist with tank-infantry co-operation to reduce the enemy position with either gunfire or flame from the armoured vehicle. The SCR-536 was introduced for use by platoon and company communication and under good conditions had a range of about a mile. With its fifty channels, SCR-536 was the first hand-held portable radio system. (*USAMHI*)

Soldiers from the US 77th Division use navy cargo nets to scale an escarpment's face. On 30 April–1 May, two platoons from Company B, 1st Battalion from the 77th Division's 307th Infantry Regiment's reached the edge of the Maeda Escarpment by nightfall. However, a Japanese counter-attack drove the men off it. In addition, on 1 May, Company A troops from this same battalion, using 50-foot scaling ladders, mounted the eastern end of the escarpment. However, enemy fire killed or wounded any American soldier who stood upright. On 3 May, other soldiers from the 307th's 1st Battalion fought to gain the top of the escarpment, but the Japanese were using grenades, grenade-dischargers ('knee mortars') and accurate mortar-fire from reverse slope positions drove the 77th's soldiers back across the escarpment's narrow top. The to-and-fro movements of both sides atop segments of the Maeda Escarpment resembled a hacksaw, hence the escarpment's moniker Hacksaw Ridge. (*NARA*)

An artillery bombardment was unleashed by Tenth Army's field regiments on the north-to-south running Yaeju-Dake Escarpment prior to the 96th Division's attack in early June. The bursts are from white phosphorus shells. This escarpment, along with the Yuza-Dake one, formed the terrain features for Ushijima's 32nd Army's last stand. On 4 June, the 96th Division was to the west of the 7th Division's movement along the eastern coastline. *(NARA)*

US 96th Division infantrymen atop the Yaeju-Dake Ridge on 18 June. Tanks and infantry moved about *(background)* while a 0.30-inch calibre Browning M1917 A1 medium machine-gun was at the ready. The light-coloured cloth *(right)* marked the American front-line to prevent aerial 'friendly fire'. Ushijima had placed the remaining 8,000 infantrymen from his 24th Division in the centre and across the western flank from Yaeju-Dake to the village of Itoman. The remnants of the 44th IMB defended the eastern part of this escarpment's line as it faced the 7th Division. *(NARA)*

(**Above**) A squad from the 6th Marine Division's Reconnaissance Company manhandles supplies and ammunition up a steep grade in order to blast Japanese caves on the island of Senaga Shima in June. During the 6th Marine Division's assault on the Oroku Peninsula, elements of the 4th Marines received 20mm cannon and heavier fire from Senaga Shima, a small rocky island less than a mile off the south-western coast of the peninsula. Gunfire from field artillery units as well as navy warships had silenced all enemy ordnance except for the 20mm cannons. The 6th Reconnaissance Company received orders on 13 June to land on and capture Senaga Shima. (*NARA*)

(**Opposite, above**) Tenth Army artillery shells Senaga Shima in early June, from the photographer's vantage point of Naha Airfield on the Oroku Peninsula's west coast. A destroyed Japanese aircraft is on the airfield (*foreground*). The 6th Reconnaissance Company plus a company from the 1st Battalion, 29th Marines, 6th Marine Division landed unopposed on Senaga Shima via LVT (A) assault on 14 June. Senaga Shima had been bombarded continuously for four days before the Marines embarked for this small East China Sea island, silencing all Japanese guns. (*NARA*)

(**Opposite, below**) A patrol from the 7th Marines, 1st Division, haul in parachuted supplies and ammunition during combat atop Kunishi Ridge on 12 June. Movement across the broad open valley approaches to the ridge was too hazardous with enemy weapons sited in. Thus, supplies were brought in by tanks or by air-drop, most of the latter falling on target into the drop-zone controlled by the Marines. (*NARA*)

A trio of 1st Division Marines attacks a Japanese limestone cave on Kunishi Ridge in mid-June. One Marine threw a grenade into the cave's opening to flush out the enemy occupants while another has his M1 Garand rifle at the ready. The 7th Marines atop the crest of Kunishi Ridge had to methodically destroy the enemy emplacements on the ridge in their attempts to gain the height entirely and close in on the village of Kunishi beyond. *(NARA)*

Epilogue

At 1300hrs on 21 June, Geiger announced Okinawa secured after eighty-two days of horrific combat. Stilwell ordered intensive 'mopping-up' on southern Okinawa on 23 June, which required an additional seven days resulting in 9,000 additional Japanese killed and 4,000 captured.

Total American battle casualties for the Okinawa campaign exceeded 49,000 with 12,520 killed or missing and 36,631 wounded. Both American and British naval forces suffered grievously at the hands of Japanese *kamikaze* attacks. Almost 5,000 American sailors were either killed or missing in action with another 4,800 wounded, making Okinawa the US Navy's single bloodiest conflict in its history. Among carrier-based aircraft, 763 Allied planes were lost in combat or to accident. Thirty-six Allied ships were sunk with another 368 damaged.

Japanese losses for the Okinawa campaign were estimated to be close to 130,000 killed with over 10,000 captured. These figures included some civilian losses. Almost 8,000 Japanese aircraft were destroyed by Allied AA fire on the ground or aboard ship. In addition, sixteen IJN warships were sunk, including the *Yamato*.

Stilwell had set a feverish pace to prepare Okinawa as a major airbase and fleet anchorage for the anticipated combat on Japan's Home Islands. The brutality of the Okinawa campaign had forecast the bloodshed that was yet to unfold. The two atomic bombs dropped at Hiroshima and Nagasaki on 6 and 9 August, respectively, erased those fears and relegated Okinawa as the Second World War's last battle. On 7 September, Stilwell negotiated the surrender of the enemy garrisons in the Ryukyus, numbering over 105,000 soldiers and sailors. The costliest and last American campaign in the Second World War had ended.

(**Opposite, above**) Japanese soldiers exit their concealed cave positions to surrender to soldiers of the 7th Division on the island's eastern coast. Beginning on 19 June, Japanese soldiers in the path of the 7th Division's advance began laying down their weapons as opposed to committing ritual suicide. (*USAMHI*)

(**Opposite, below**) Within the 7th Division front, American interpreters and psychological warfare units were using armour-mounted loudspeakers to induce the remaining enemy soldiers to surrender. Here, a captured Japanese soldier is using a hand-held microphone to exhort his fellow soldiers to surrender rather than continue fighting or committing suicide. Some Okinawan inhabitants are seen (*left*). (*NARA*)

(**Above**) Two Marines hold fire on an elderly man exiting from a concealed location at the close of hostilities. He was probably an Okinawan native. However, on 19 June, Ushijima had exhorted most of his staff officers to disguise themselves as native islanders and infiltrate Tenth Army lines to escape to the northern part of the island. (*NARA*)

(**Above**) Lieutenant Milton Sorem, USNR, attached to the 77th Division, is shown escorting three Okinawan children through the mud past an LVT towards American lines after the capture of Shuri in early June. (*USAMHI*)

(**Opposite, above**) A seemingly content group of IJN personnel surrender to Marines from the 2nd Battalion, 29th Marines, 6th Division near the Oroku Peninsula's sea-wall mid-June. The young boy (*second from left*) was an Okinawan 'Youth Corps' draftee. The 29th Marines made the final sweep of the remaining Japanese-held area near the Kokuba Estuary's marshy grasslands. On 14 June, Marine riflemen reached the sea-wall to ferret out the last of the enemy in the cane fields and rice paddies near the river. In all, seventy-eight Japanese prisoners were taken that day while over 800 IJN combatants preferred combat death or suicide. (*NARA*)

(**Opposite, below**) A 6th Division Marine views the ruins of Naha from a gaping hole in the wall of a previous theatre in early June. After the city's bombardment, only the skeletons of the city's buildings remained. Before the island's invasion, Naha had a population of over 60,000 inhabitants from the island's estimated pre-war population of 435,000. (*USMC*)

(**Opposite, above**) The corpse of Lieutenant-General Simon Bolivar Buckner, Jr is carried from an ambulance into a tent after he had been mortally wounded at the front-lines. Buckner, after being warned about Japanese activity in the area, was observing 8th Marines' tank-infantry movements from a coral boulder ridge position at the front on 18 June. A Navy doctor and corpsman administered plasma at the site, but Buckner died from extensive blood loss. (*NARA*)

(**Opposite, below**) The USS *New Mexico* bursts into flames after a *kamikaze's* impact at dusk on 12 May, as viewed from the deck of the USS *Wichita*. US Navy casualties during the entire campaign were more than 4,900 killed and missing with another 4,800 wounded. (*NARA*)

(**Above**) The extremely grim scene of a Marine tying down the bodies of his comrades killed in combat onto a truck for burial. Marine infantry casualties among the 1st and 6th Marine Divisions, along with the late attachment of elements of the 8th Marines, 2nd Division, as well as air-crew losses were almost 3,000 dead and missing along with more than 13,000 wounded. (*NARA*)

(**Opposite, above**) An army chaplain conducts a burial service for 27th Division's soldiers killed during XXIV Corps' campaign. This division, which started out the campaign as a floating reserve offshore of eastern Okinawa, eventually suffered more than 700 soldiers killed in action with over 2,500 wounded. The other XXIV Corps divisions, the 7th, 77th and 96th Infantries, lost almost 4,000 soldiers killed in action with another 15,000 wounded. (*NARA*)

(**Opposite, below**) Sixty-two seamen from the ship's ranks of the USS *Hancock*, one of twenty-four Essex-class aircraft carriers built during the war, have their bodies committed to the deep waters of the East China Sea after a Japanese *kamikaze* attack on 7 April. While almost 400 US Navy aerial sorties on the IJN battleship *Yamato*, the light cruiser *Yahagi* and four IJN destroyers were underway that day, a Japanese suicide plane dropped its bomb from a height of 50 feet onto the flight deck of the *Hancock* before intentionally crashing into some parked planes to the aft of the vessel. Another seventy-one seamen of the carrier's complement were wounded. Heroic efforts by the ship's crew put out the inferno and the *Hancock* was back in action within an hour. More than fifty Japanese *kamikaze* planes were shot down by TF 58 on the morning of 7 April alone. (*NARA*)

(**Above**) Lieutenant-General Joseph W. Stilwell, commanding general Ryukyu Command (formerly Tenth Army), is seated, signing the official surrender document of IJA and IJN forces in the Ryukyus on 7 September. To the right of Stilwell is Brigadier-General Frank D. Merrill, who served in Burma as the commander of 'Merrill's Marauders', who were vital at combating the IJA 18th Army in northern Burma during the 1944 Sino-American offensive that seized the Japanese airfield at Myitkyina in a *coup de main* attack led by Merrill's deputy, Colonel Charles Hunter, on 17 May. Standing behind Stilwell are the IJA and IJN senior officers who were ordered to report from their various remaining Ryukyu Islands garrisons for the formal surrender ceremony. (*NARA*)

The author's late father, Maurice Diamond, to whom this book is dedicated. He was a radar operator assigned to a Baltimore-class heavy cruiser during the closing weeks of the Second World War. He returned home after his service to raise a family and contribute to a revitalised post-war United States, as did millions of other countries' veterans across the globe. His youthful visage saddens me, though, as I realise that so many other young men and women died or were grievously wounded too early in their lives in order to end the brutal global conflagration. (*Author's Collection*)

References

Appleman, Roy E., **Burns**, James M., **Gugeler**, Russell A. and **Stevens**, John. *Okinawa: The Last Battle*. Barnes & Noble, New York, 1995.

Diamond, Jon. *Guadalcanal. The American Campaign against Japan in WWII*. Stackpole Books, Guilford, 2017.

Diamond, Jon. *New Guinea. The Allied Jungle Campaign in World War II*. Stackpole Books, Guilford, 2015.

Diamond, Jon. *The War in the South Pacific*. Pen & Sword Books, Barnsley, 2017.

Frank, Benis M. *Okinawa. Touchstone to Victory*. Ballantine's Illustrated History of World War II. Ballantine Books, New York, 1969.

Frank, Benis M. and **Shaw**, Henry I, Jr. *Victory and Occupation. History of US Marine Corps in World War II. Volume V.* US Government Printing Office, Washington, DC, 1968.

Leckie, Robert. *Okinawa. The Last Battle of World War II*. Penguin Books, New York, 1996.

Morison, Samuel Eliot. *History of the United States Naval Operations in World War II. Vol. XIV Victory in the Pacific, 1945*. Castle Books, Edison, 2001.

Rottman, Gordon L. *Okinawa 1945. The Last Battle*. Osprey Publishing, Oxford, 2002.

Sloan, Bill. *The Ultimate Battle. Okinawa 1945 – The Last Epic Struggle of World War II*. Simon and Schuster, New York, 2008.

Wheeler, Richard. *A Special Valor. The U.S. Marines & the Pacific War*. Castle Books. Edison, 1996.

Yahara, Hiromichi. *The Battle for Okinawa*. John Wiley & Sons, Inc. New York, 1995.

Notes

Notes

Notes